Getting Started with Unity 5

Leverage the power of Unity 5 to create
amazing 3D games

Dr. Edward Lavieri

BIRMINGHAM - MUMBAI

Getting Started with Unity 5

First published: May 2015

Production reference: 1250515

Published by Packt Publishing Ltd.
Livery Place
35 Livery Street
Birmingham B3 2PB, UK.

ISBN 978-1-78439-831-6

www.packtpub.com

Credits

Author
Dr. Edward Lavieri

Reviewers
Maxim Jankov
Adam Larson
Michael E. Miles

Commissioning Editor
Ashwin Nair

Acquisition Editor
Nikhil Karkal

Content Development Editor
Shweta Pant

Technical Editors
Rosmy George
Ankita Thakur

Copy Editors
Sonia Michelle Cheema
Ameesha Green

Project Coordinator
Shipra Chawhan

Proofreaders
Stephen Copestake
Safis Editing

Indexer
Monica Ajmera Mehta

Graphics
Sheetal Aute

Production Coordinator
Arvindkumar Gupta

Cover Work
Arvindkumar Gupta

About the Author

Dr. Edward Lavieri is a veteran game designer and developer with a strong academic background. He earned a doctorate of computer science from Colorado Technical University, and three masters of science degrees in management information systems from Bowie State University. His formal education includes instructional design (from Capella University) and operations management (from the University of Arkansas), demonstrating his passion for academic pursuits. He has developed and taught computer-related courses since 2002 and currently teaches at Southern New Hampshire University. Edward retired from the US Navy after 25 years as an intelligence specialist and command master chief.

As the founder and creative director of three19, a software design and development studio, Edward is constantly developing software. He uses Unity as one of his primary game development tools. He focuses on developing adaptive learning systems, educational games, and mobile apps.

Edward authored *Adaptive Learning for Educational Game Design, CreateSpace Independent Publishing Platform, LiveCode Mobile Development HOTSHOT, Packt Publishing, LiveCode Mobile Development Cookbook, Packt Publishing, Software Consulting: A Revolutionary Approach, CreateSpace Independent Publishing Platform*, and was the technical editor of *Excel Formulas and Functions for Dummies, Ken Bluttman, Wiley Publishing*. He has also developed numerous college courses, involving computer science and information systems.

I would like to thank Colt for always bringing a smile to my face and heart. To Noel and Josh, thank you for being in my life and creating Colt. I love all three of you. My deepest appreciation and love goes to Brenda. You are my world and let me tell you, I do love living in it. I would like to express my gratitude to Fuel So Good Coffee Roasters for fueling my writing and game development. I would also like to thank the expert team at Packt Publishing, including Harshit, Owen, Govindan, Shweta, Nikhil, the reviewers, technical editors, proofreaders, indexers, and the marketing team. It is a pleasure to have worked with such an amazing team.

About the Reviewers

Adam Larson has been programming since 2001. His first venture into the game industry started as a programmer, working on digital downloadable titles for Xbox Live Arcade. Since then, he has worked on titles on every modern platform. Adam discovered Unity about 5 years ago, and has been a huge advocate of it as it has grown into the powerhouse it is today.

He currently manages Zymo Entertainment, a small start-up located near Green Bay, Wisconsin. The company focuses on business applications using Unity 3D as well as video games.

> I really want to thank my coworkers at Zymo Entertainment, as they've let me bounce a few ideas off of them.

Michael E. Miles purchased his first computer in 1979 and since then, he has been hooked on to programming, specifically at the machine language level. The Z80 (TRS80) and 6502 (Apple II) microprocessors were top-of-the-line processors at that time, and he began programming by creating custom commands for each of the BASIC languages of these machines. As the graphic capabilities of PCs increased, his interest in graphics and animation took over with the introduction of AutoCAD. Combining his love for computer graphics and aircrafts, he became an aerospace manufacturing engineer, creating visual/animated fabrication and installation instructions for the manufacture of aircraft structures. To formulate these instructions, he frequently uses CATIA, Blender, After Effects, and has recently been incorporating game engines into his workflows, specifically, Unity and Unreal Engine 4. Michael currently works for various aerospace companies in the aerospace and defense industry as a contract manufacturing engineer, and is originally from Seattle, Washington.

www.PacktPub.com

Support files, eBooks, discount offers, and more

For support files and downloads related to your book, please visit www.PacktPub.com.

Did you know that Packt offers eBook versions of every book published, with PDF and ePub files available? You can upgrade to the eBook version at www.PacktPub.com and as a print book customer, you are entitled to a discount on the eBook copy. Get in touch with us at service@packtpub.com for more details.

At www.PacktPub.com, you can also read a collection of free technical articles, sign up for a range of free newsletters and receive exclusive discounts and offers on Packt books and eBooks.

https://www2.packtpub.com/books/subscription/packtlib

Do you need instant solutions to your IT questions? PacktLib is Packt's online digital book library. Here, you can search, access, and read Packt's entire library of books.

Why subscribe?

- Fully searchable across every book published by Packt
- Copy and paste, print, and bookmark content
- On demand and accessible via a web browser

Free access for Packt account holders

If you have an account with Packt at www.PacktPub.com, you can use this to access PacktLib today and view 9 entirely free books. Simply use your login credentials for immediate access.

Table of Contents

Preface

With the pervasiveness of games and the use of gamification in nearly every industry, the desire to discover how to use state of the art development software has never been so great. There is an increasing number of software tools available to help developers create amazing games for consoles, the Web, desktop computers, and mobile devices. Game engines are among the most powerful of these tools available. The Unity 3D game engine is one of the elite game engines. It has been used to create popular 2D and 3D games by large game studios and indie developers. With a free version available, and the release of Unity 5, the time has never been better to start using Unity.

Getting Started with Unity 5 covers one of the most popular game engines available. This book will guide you through the entire process of creating a 3D game, from downloading the Unity game engine to publishing your game. You will enjoy having complete coverage of exciting topics including player-controlled characters and animation. Whether you are just getting started as a game developer or have experience with Unity or other game engines, this book will provide you with a guided tour of developing games with Unity 5. With clear explanations, tips, and ample screenshots, you will be provided with detailed steps to develop your game.

This book takes a practice hands-on approach to learning Unity 5. As you progress through each chapter, you will build a 3D interactive game called *Little Farmer Colt*. As you create the game, you'll learn key features of Unity 5 including creating a game environment, animating characters, scripting, and more. All meshes, models, textures, animations, and other assets are available on the book's website.

By the time you complete the lessons in this book, you'll have full confidence to start using Unity 5 to create your own games.

What this book covers

Chapter 1, Getting Jiggy with the Unity Interface, surveys the game engine landscape, comparing other game engines with Unity to give you a full appreciation for Unity's capabilities. You'll learn how to download and install Unity 5. You'll also learn about Unity 5's user interface and core tools, including transform tools and cameras.

Chapter 2, Creating the Game Environment, will teach you about game design by reviewing the book's game design of *Little Farmer Colt*. You'll start creating the game environment with terrain, mountains, trees, a lake, and the sky.

Chapter 3, Working with Assets, is all about the assets used to develop games with Unity 5. You'll learn about assets, where to get them, how to make your own, and how to import them into your game. You'll also learn about free 3D object creation software to create game objects compatible with Unity 5.

Chapter 4, Animating the Game Characters, is about Unity animations and player controllers. You'll see our game characters come to life and give your users the ability to control the player.

Chapter 5, Scripting the Game, is dedicated to teaching you how to script. You'll start with a primer on C# and experience with MonoDevelop. You'll also gain experience creating your own C# scripts for your game.

Chapter 6, Adding a Graphical User Interface, contains key information on graphical user interfaces and their importance to games. You'll gain hands-on experience with the Unity 5 user interface system. You'll learn to create a heads-up display, an in-game mini-map, and full-screen navigation menus.

Chapter 7, Polishing and Optimizing the Game, will teach you several ways to make your game shine and operate optimally. You'll gain appreciation for the importance of audio and visual effects in games and how to create them. You'll gain experience with sound effects, shadows, lighting effects, and camera rendering. You'll also learn about optimizing scripts.

Chapter 8, What's Next?, is the final chapter where you'll receive several specific suggestions on how to take the *Little Farmer Colt* game to a higher level. You'll also learn about Unity workflow, project scalability, cross-platform issues, and the importance of attribution. You'll also gain an appreciation for advanced topics.

What you need for this book

In order to follow the examples in this book, you'll need a copy of Unity 5 or greater. This software is available for free at `http://unity3d.com/get-unity/download`. You can use up-to-date Windows or Mac operating systems. You'll also need an Internet connection to download the graphic assets presented in this book.

Who this book is for

This book is written for people new to Unity or that have some experience with a version prior to Unity 5. If you want to take a look at Unity 5, get a refresher, or just want to see how games can be developed with a top game engine, this book is for you.

Conventions

In this book, you will find a number of styles of text that distinguish between different kinds of information. Here are some examples of these styles, and an explanation of their meaning.

Code words in text, database table names, folder names, filenames, file extensions, pathnames, dummy URLs, user input, and Twitter handles are shown as follows: "In that folder, you'll find four subfolders titled `Assets`, `Library`, `ProjectSettings`, and `Temp`."

A block of code is set as follows:

```
public class EatCorn : MonoBehavior {

    void Start ( ) {
    }

    void Update ( ) {
    }
}
```

New terms and **important words** are shown in bold. Words that you see on the screen, in menus or dialog boxes for example, appear in the text like this: "You will see a **Download** link at the top-right section of the web page."

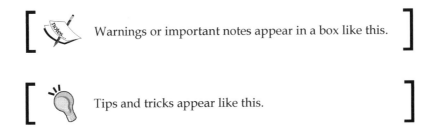

Warnings or important notes appear in a box like this.

Tips and tricks appear like this.

Reader feedback

Feedback from our readers is always welcome. Let us know what you think about this book—what you liked or disliked. Reader feedback is important for us as it helps us develop titles that you will really get the most out of.

To send us general feedback, simply e-mail feedback@packtpub.com, and mention the book's title in the subject of your message.

If there is a topic that you have expertise in and you are interested in either writing or contributing to a book, see our author guide at www.packtpub.com/authors.

Customer support

Now that you are the proud owner of a Packt book, we have a number of things to help you to get the most from your purchase.

Downloading the example code

You can download the example code files for all Packt books you have purchased from your account at http://www.packtpub.com. If you purchased this book elsewhere, you can visit http://www.packtpub.com/support and register to have the files e-mailed directly to you.

Downloading the color images of this book

We also provide you with a PDF file that has color images of the screenshots/diagrams used in this book. The color images will help you better understand the changes in the output. You can download this file from: http://www.packtpub.com/sites/default/files/downloads/8316OT_ColorImages.pdf.

Errata

Although we have taken every care to ensure the accuracy of our content, mistakes do happen. If you find a mistake in one of our books—maybe a mistake in the text or the code—we would be grateful if you could report this to us. By doing so, you can save other readers from frustration and help us improve subsequent versions of this book. If you find any errata, please report them by visiting http://www.packtpub.com/submit-errata, selecting your book, clicking on the **Errata Submission Form** link, and entering the details of your errata. Once your errata are verified, your submission will be accepted and the errata will be uploaded to our website or added to any list of existing errata under the Errata section of that title.

To view the previously submitted errata, go to https://www.packtpub.com/books/content/support and enter the name of the book in the search field. The required information will appear under the **Errata** section.

Piracy

Piracy of copyrighted material on the Internet is an ongoing problem across all media. At Packt, we take the protection of our copyright and licenses very seriously. If you come across any illegal copies of our works in any form on the Internet, please provide us with the location address or website name immediately so that we can pursue a remedy.

Please contact us at copyright@packtpub.com with a link to the suspected pirated material.

We appreciate your help in protecting our authors and our ability to bring you valuable content.

Questions

If you have a problem with any aspect of this book, you can contact us at questions@packtpub.com, and we will do our best to address the problem.

1
Getting Jiggy with the Unity Interface

The purpose of this chapter is to familiarize you with Unity and its interface. We'll start with a discussion of game engines to see how Unity stacks up. You'll be guided through the download and installation process. We'll then discuss the Unity project and its file structure in and out of Unity.

We'll also take a look at the Unity interface. We'll experiment with different layouts to give you an idea of the different workflows you can set up. I'll explain each view in Unity and discuss the purpose of each one. We'll spend extra time in the **Scene** view using the transform tools, so that you'll be comfortable using them. This chapter will end with a discussion on how cameras are used in Unity.

Through this chapter, you will:

- Understand the Unity engine
- Be able to download and install Unity
- Understand the Unity projects
- Be comfortable with the Unity layouts
- Understand the purpose of each view
- Be able to navigate using the **Scene** view
- Be familiar with the transform tools
- Be familiar with Cameras

Why Unity?

There are several dozen game engines available for 2D and 3D game development. So why choose Unity? I probably do not have to convince you of that because you are reading this book. In case you still need convincing, let me tell you about some of the competition, first.

Unreal and CryEngine are among the most capable game engines available. Large game studios have created 3D games using these game engines for many years. Both engines have been used to create high-grossing games. The pricing models and complexities of using them are enough to make indie game developers and small game development studios look the other way.

What about easy-to-use game engines? Game Salad, Game Maker, and Construct 2 are all easy to learn and use. In fact, you can create simple games with these engines without having to program or script a single line of code. These are all 2D game development engines and lack the capabilities of the larger engines.

This does not put Unity in the middle of the easy-to-use and most capable game engines. Along the spectrum of capabilities, **Unity** is to the far right. See the following diagram:

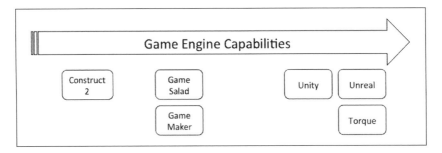

Let's review the following table so that these game engines can be compared based on their capabilities, learning curve, and what programming languages are used to develop games with each engine:

Game Engine	Learning Curve	Language	2D/3D
Unity	4 of 5	C#, JS, Boo	Both
Unreal	5 of 5	C++	3D
CryEngine	5 of 5	C++, Lua	Both
Game Salad	1 of 5	GML	2D
Game Maker	1 of 5	N/A	2D
Construct 2	2 of 5	JS	2D

The Unity game engine sits in a sweet spot between tremendous capabilities and difficulty to learn. This makes it the engine of choice for many developers. As you'll see later in this chapter, we declare either 2D or 3D when we create a game project. There are some other beneficial reasons for using Unity over the other game engines:

- The ability to program with C#, JavaScript, Boo, or any combination of these languages in the same game.

> While Unity supports scripts in the different supported languages (C#, JavaScript, and Boo) in the same game, I do not recommend this. The best practice is to pick a single programming language and use it throughout the game.

- The ability to test play games in a separate view (window) without having to create builds or leave the development interface

- The ability to make changes to the game while it is being played and not having those changes impact on the saved version. This is a great way to experiment and test.

- The ability to develop once and then deploy to mobile (iOS, Android, Windows Phone 8, and BlackBerry 10), desktop (Mac, Windows, and Linux), Web (Safari, Firefox, Chrome, and Internet Explorer), and console devices (Xbox One, Xbox 360, PlayStation 3, PlayStation 4, PlayStation Vita, and Wii U).

In addition to these great reasons to select Unity as your game engine of choice, it is free for most purposes. There is a Pro version that costs money, but if you want to get started without having to spend any money, Unity is for you.

Getting your hands on Unity

If you already have Unity installed on your computer, you can skip this section. Otherwise, you can follow the steps in this section to download and install Unity on your computer:

1. Go to the Unity home page: `http://www.unity3d.com`.

2. You see a **Download** link at the top-right section of the web page. Click that link to go to Unity's download page, as shown in the following screenshot:

3. On the download page, you'll see a **Download Unity** button that includes the current version of the engine. For example, the button might say **Download Unity 5.1**. The web page will know what operating system your computer has and will download the correct version. Click on the **Download** button. The installation file is quite large, well over 1GB, and could take several minutes to download, especially if you have a slow Internet connection.

4. Once the download completes, simply double-click on the `installation` file and let the installer do the work. Accept any defaults if prompted. Unity is an industrial strength game engine, so do not be alarmed if the installation process takes a while.

5. Now you are ready to launch Unity for the first time. Double-click on the **Unity** icon.

Projects

The first thing we must do to use Unity is to create a project. Just like word processing software using a document to create a letter, Unity uses projects to create games. Projects are the enveloping structure for all the scripts, game objects, art, and other source files that are used in a game. You'll see later in this chapter how the external file structure of project files is replicated in Unity.

When Unity is launched, the first screen you should see is the welcome screen window, as shown in the following screenshot:

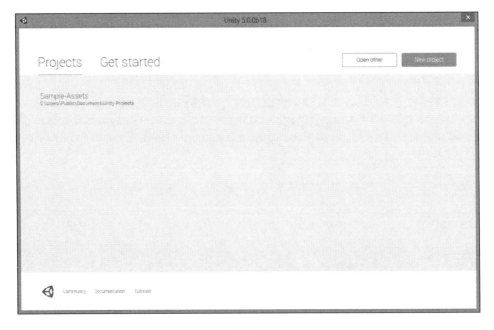

From this dialog window, you can easily open projects that you've recently worked on; they'll be listed on the left under the **Projects** link. You can also open a new project by clicking on the **New project** button in the upper-right section of the window.

Let's walk through creating a new project. Our first step is to click on the **New project** button. This brings up the new project dialog window, as shown in the following screenshot:

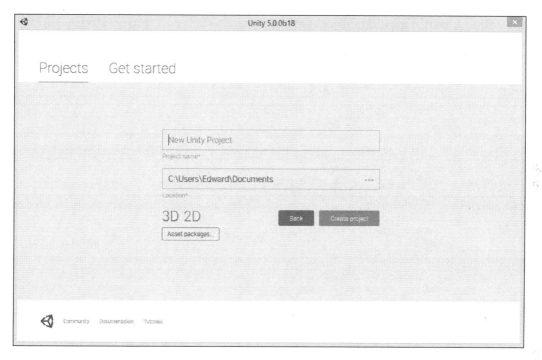

There are four decisions you need to make on this screen before you click on the **Create project** button. First, you'll need to give your project a name. This is like naming a file, and I recommend including the version number. For example, if you are working on the first version of a new game called **Java For Everyone**, you might name your project Java4Everyone 1.0, java_for_everyone_1.0, or something similar.

The next step is to tell Unity where you want the project saved. You can accept the default or click on the eclipse icon to open a **File Explorer** window. Using this window, select where you want your project to be saved. I recommend selecting a folder or directory that is automatically backed up or linked to a cloud-based file system. This will help to ensure that you do not lose your work.

Next, we need to indicate whether we are creating a 2D or 3D project. If you are creating a platform or side-scrolling game, you'll select 2D. Otherwise, you'll select 3D. You can certainly have both 2D and 3D components to your game. Unity gives us a lot of flexibility in this regard. So, our initial selection simply indicates our primary focus.

Our last decision to make is what, if any, asset packages we want to import. If you already know what packages you will need, you can have them loaded when the project is created. Alternatively, you can easily import packages after you've started working on your project. This is the method I recommend because it ensures you only load what you absolutely need. We'll discuss how this is done in a later chapter.

Once you've made the four decisions, click on the **Create project** button, as shown in the following screenshot:

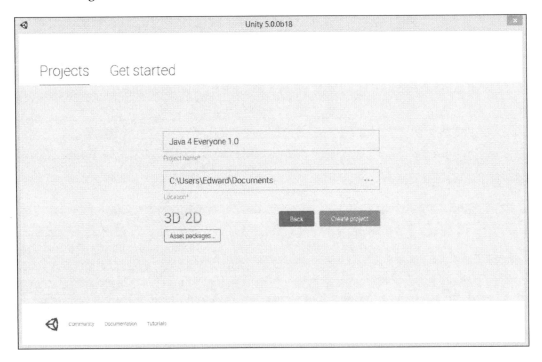

Unity will create your project and depending on how many packages you selected to be included, it could take more than a few seconds to create. If the window disappears and you do not see any indication that your project is being created, don't panic. Unity is working in the background and will open the main interface as soon as the project has been created.

If you look at your filesystem, you'll see that Unity has created a folder with the name of your project. In that folder, you'll find four subfolders titled `Assets`, `Library`, `ProjectSettings`, and `Temp`. Unity keeps projects well organized with these primary folders. As new game objects are added to your project, they will be placed in these folders. You can also create additional folders to be even more organized.

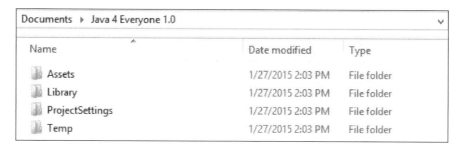

It is a good idea not to move files around or change folder names. There is a chance you'll break linkages inside your project. Instead, make any desired changes within Unity.

Layouts

One of the wonderful things about working with Unity is that you can customize the way the user interface is laid out. You can use one of the predefined layouts of **2 by 3**, **4 Split**, **Tall**, or **Wide**, or you can create your own. Layouts refer to how the various views in Unity are arranged on the screen. You'll learn about views in the next section.

To change a layout, we simply click on the **Layout** button that is located in the far top-right corner of the Unity interface:

Let's look at each layout to see the differences. The first layout is the 2 by 3 layout. This layout provides a nice arrangement with the **Scene** and **Game** views on the left, the **Hierarchy** and **Project** views in the middle and a full **Inspector** view on the right, as shown in the following screenshot:

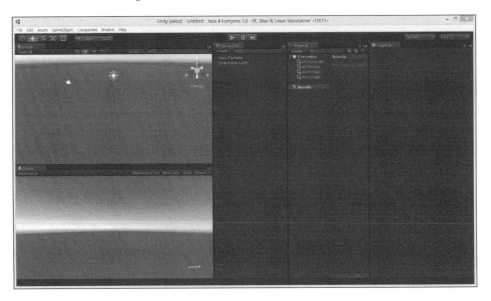

The **4 Split** layout provides four different views of the same scene, as shown in the following screenshot. This is a good way to review how lighting and shading is implemented in your game. We'll talk about lighting and shading later in the book.

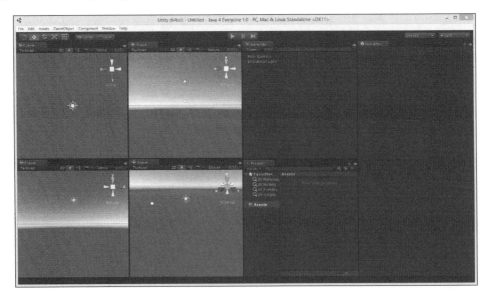

The **Tall** layout provides a tall, but not wide view of the **Scene** view with other views located on the right, as shown in the following screenshot:

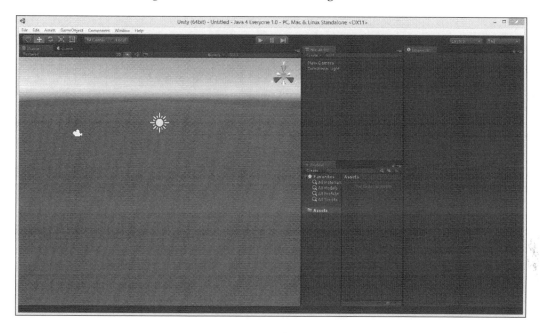

The **Wide** layout provides a wide view of the **Scene** view, with other views located on the bottom and on the right, as shown in the following screenshot:

The **Default** layout is a variation of the **Wide** layout. The difference is that with the **Default** layout, the **Hierarchy** view is on the left, as shown in the following screenshot:

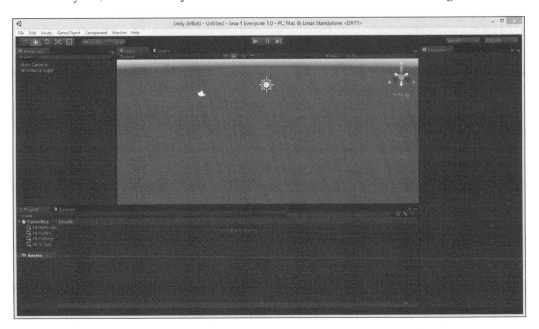

You can switch between views anytime you want without it impacting your game. Most Unity developers do not work in just one view. Different views provide different benefits and are appropriate for different tasks. You can also modify any view by dragging any of the borders of a view. If you want to save a view, make any changes to the current view, then select the **Layout** button and select **Save Layout**. You will be prompted for a name.

Views

Unity views provide the ability to see, or view, specific components of the project. There are five views in Unity.

The Scene view

Scenes in Unity are the equivalent to levels in a game. You'll have a different scene for every game level. The **Scene** view is where we put visual objects such as characters, buildings, terrain, and more. We can also move, rotate, and scale these objects in the **Scene** view by using transform tools, which we'll discuss in the next section. Take a look at the following screenshot:

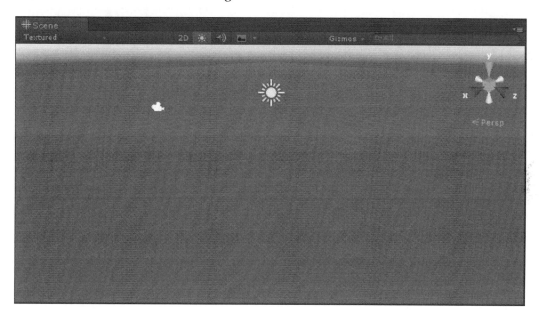

The Game view

One of the great features of Unity is that we can play our game right in the game engine. This means we do not need to compile the game and play it outside of Unity. If you're already a game developer, you'll appreciate the time saving. The **Game** view is where the game is played during development.

Any changes made to the game while the game is being played will be reflected in the game but are not saved when gameplay ends. This represents a wonderful way to experiment and not risk breaking scripts or other game components.

Like with most games, Unity games are played from a player's perspective. Typically, a player controls an in-game character. We do not see the game world through the in-game character's eyes. It might seem that way, but we are actually seeing the game world as rendered by a camera or cameras. We'll talk more about this later. For now, think of a camera hovering just above and behind our in-game character's head. This makes it seem like we are seeing through their eyes:

The Hierarchy view

This view displays a hierarchical list of every object in the scene. When you double-click on an object in this view, two things happen. First, the object is selected and viewable in the **Scene** view. Unity orients the **Scene** view so that the selected object is in the front and center. The second thing that happens is that the **Inspector** view is populated to display the selected object's settings and components. You'll gain great exposure to this later in the book. Take a look at the options shown in the following screenshot:

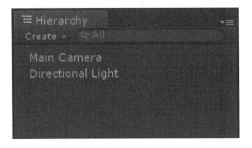

The Project view

The **Project** view provides us with a file structure of our game components including objects, art, scripts, and so on. The file structure here is what is displayed on your system's file structure. So, if you want to make changes, do it in the **Project** view, not directly on your computer. You'll notice that this view has two columns. The first column contains the file structure I mentioned as well as **Favorites**, which will help you to find assets quickly. This is especially handy for large projects.

The second column contains folder contents. If, for example, you click on a folder in the left **Project** view column, that folder's contents will be displayed in the second column. You can drag objects directly from this view into the **Scene** view to add objects to your game. I'll walk you through this later in the book. Take a look at the options shown in the following screenshot:

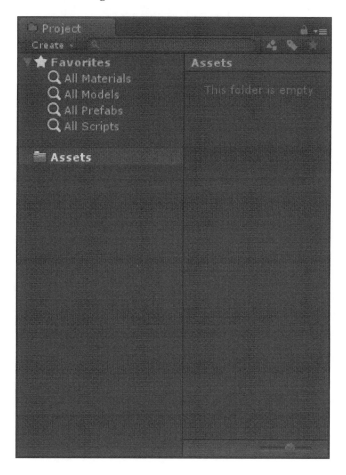

The Inspector view

When objects are selected in another view, their details are revealed in the **Inspector** view. In many cases, you can make changes to an object directly in the **Inspector** view. You'll be doing this a lot throughout the book.

Remember, layouts are made up of views and you have complete control over how the interface is laid out. For the majority of this book, I'll use the 2 x 3 layout because of its utility. You can use any view you want and will still be able to follow along with the instructions and guides provided in the rest of this book.

Transform tools

Transform tools in Unity allow us to interact with the **Scene** view, edit terrain, move objects, and make modifications. There are five buttons that make up the transform tools, as shown in the following screenshot; they are located in the top-left corner of the Unity Interface:

The first button is the **Hand** tool or **View** Tool ( ). When this tool is selected, our cursor in the **Scene** view turns to a hand. This lets us know what mode we are in. With this tool selected, we can scroll with our mouse to zoom in and out of the scene. If you click on the left mouse button, you are able to pan around the scene. With the right mouse button clicked, you are able to look around based on the current position of your cursor.

If you hold down the *Alt* key on a PC or *Option* key on a Mac and click on the left mouse button, you can orbit around the current area. Pressing that same key and the right mouse button allows you to zoom in and out of the scene.

The second button is the **Translate** tool ( ) and is in the shape of a quad arrow. When an object selected and then click on the translate tool, the object will have three gizmos, one for each axis. Clicking and dragging any of these gizmos moves the object along the respective access, as shown in the following screenshot:

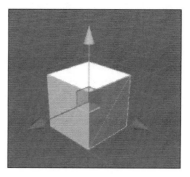

The third transform tool is the **Rotate** tool ( ), which looks like two rotating arrows. This tool allows us to rotate an object along any axis (x, y, or z). Instead of line and arrow gizmos, this tool is instantiated with three colored rings, one for each axis. Clicking a ring and dragging it rotates the object along that axis, as shown in the following screenshot:

The fourth transform tool is the **Scale** tool (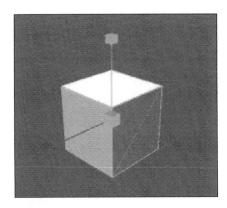), which is represented with line and block gizmos. Like the other transform tools, there is one gizmo for each axis. Clicking and dragging one of these gizmos increases or decreases the object along the selected axis. For example, you can make a cube wider, narrower, taller, or shorter. If you want to maintain aspect ratio, you can click on the center square instead of the red, blue, or green square. Now, when you click-and-drag, your object will grow or shrink in perfect aspect ratio, as shown in the following screenshot:

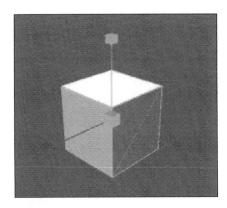

The final transform tool is the **Rect** tool (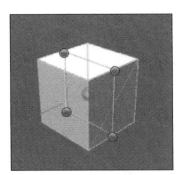) and is represented by a rectangle with intersecting points. The **Rect** tool can be used to move, resize, and rotate an object in the **Scene** view. So, this is a versatile tool that also has corresponding properties that you can edit directly using the **Inspector** view. Take a look at the following screenshot:

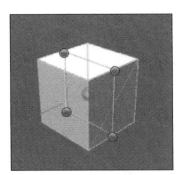

Cameras

Cameras render scenes so that the user can view them. Every scene must have at least one camera. In fact, when a new scene is created, Unity creates a camera named **Main Camera**. As you'll see later in this book, a scene can have multiple cameras. In the **Scene** view, cameras are indicated with a white camera silhouette, as shown in the following screenshot:

Cameras are game objects and can be edited using transform tools as well as in the **Inspector** view. We can classify Unity cameras based on their projection. A perspective projection camera renders a scene based on the camera angle, as it exists in the scene.

The other project is orthographic. An orthographic perspective camera renders a scene uniformly without any perspective. This type of camera is commonly used for top-down games and is the default camera used in 2D and Unity's **User Interface (UI)** system.

When a camera is selected in the **Hierarchy** view, its frustum is visible in **Scene** view. A frustum is a geographic shape that looks like a pyramid that has had its top cut off. The top plane is parallel to its base, in other words, the near and far plane.

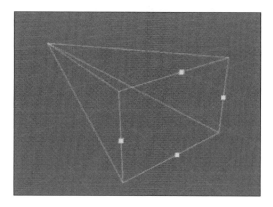

We'll use cameras in our game later in the book.

[

There are additional user interface components to Unity that we did not cover. As we need them in the development of our game, they'll be introduced prior to use.
]

Summary

In this chapter, we took a quick look at and compared game engines. We also took a closer look at Unity and reviewed some of its key features. We downloaded and installed Unity so that we're ready to start developing games. We discussed Unity projects and created one in order to become comfortable with the process. To close out the chapter, we walked through the Unity interface including looking at layouts, views, transform tools, and cameras.

In the next chapter, we'll start designing the game we'll be making through this book and you'll learn how to create the game environment.

2
Creating the Game Environment

In the last chapter, we surveyed game engines, installed Unity, and became familiar with the user interface. We're almost ready to start creating our game. Before we do, we have two tasks to attend to: designing our game and creating the game's environment. We'll handle both of these tasks in this chapter.

This chapter will set the stage for developing our game using Unity. We'll start by examining our game's design, which will serve as the blueprint we'll follow throughout the rest of this book. Next, we'll create our game's environment, which will include terrain, water, and the sky. Our terrain will consist of trees, mountains, and a river.

Through this chapter, you will:

- Understand the purpose of a game design
- Be able to create terrain in Unity
- Be familiar with using textures
- Be comfortable with creating mountains
- Be comfortable planting trees
- Be familiar with creating bodies of water
- Be able to create a sky in Unity

Game design

A game's design is like a blueprint for a house. You would not consider building a house without a blueprint and it is an equally bad idea to develop a game without designing it first. Our game design will document the look of our game, what the player's objectives are, what the gameplay will be, supported user actions, the required artificial intelligence, and game flow.

Designing a game is significantly more complex than simply considering these six elements. We do not have time to go through the entire game design process, so you'll see the primary areas of the game designed in this chapter.

Our game will be called **Little Farmer Colt**. It will feature a young farmer named Colt, who has to manage a farm. Let's look at the elements of game look, player objectives, gameplay, user actions, artificial intelligence, and end state.

Game look

All games have a look to them. For a game that takes place in space, the game look might be a futuristic/mechanical. If it is a children's math game, it might have a cartoon style look. The importance of addressing a game's look is to ensure it is consistent throughout the game.

Our game will take place on a small farm, so the game look will be rural farming. It will consist of farm animals, appropriate buildings, crops, water, grass, and dirt. One trick in maintaining game look consistency is to have the same graphic artist create all the artwork. On large projects, this is not always feasible, but it will work for our small game project. All the art used in our game was created by a single graphic artist.

Player objectives

Users that play our game will need to know what their objectives are. These objectives will give them a purpose in the game. Objectives also add fun to games. Our game will include three objectives:

- **Objective 1**: Learn how to farm the land. The player will accomplish this objective by talking to the old farmer.

- **Objective 2**: Raise chickens. This will be accomplished by gathering corn and water and feeding the chickens.

- **Objective 3**: Raise pigs. The player will meet this objective in the same manner as with the chickens: by providing food and water.

To support these objectives, we'll provide cornfields and a stream. The player will harvest corn from the fields and collect water from the stream. Both corn and water will be used to feed the farm animals.

Gameplay

Gameplay is a reference to how players interact with a game. For our Little Farmer Colt game, players will use both the keyboard and the mouse. The mouse will be used to rotate Colt; the main game character and the keyboard arrow keys will be used to navigate Colt in our game world.

The following image is a graphic view of our controls. They are standard and Unity makes it easy to use these controls. We'll take care of this later in the book:

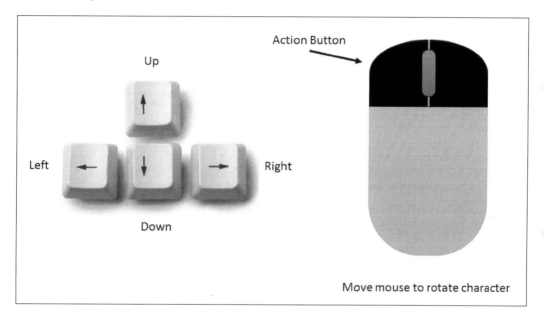

User actions

Another element of game design is defining what actions players will be able to perform. These actions might include sailing a ship, launching a rocket, swimming, climbing, and more. For our game, our player will be able to perform the following actions:

- Walk throughout the game world
- Pick up corn
- Pick up water

- Feed chickens
- Feed pigs
- Talk to the old farmer

This list of actions can serve as a checklist for things we need to implement in our game. We'll do just that later in the book.

Artificial Intelligence

Artificial Intelligence (AI) is achieved when we program game objects based on real objects that exhibit intelligence. The player will control Colt, the game character, so that just leaves a couple of game objects that we can implement AI for. These objects are the old farmer, chickens, and pigs.

We'll use the old farmer to demonstrate a dialog system. So, he will not have any AI; rather, he will have a predefined set of responses based on Colt's dialog menu selections.

Both the chickens and pigs will have similar AI implemented. They will start out as baby chicks and piglets. Given enough water and corn, they'll grow into adulthood. When fully grown, they will automatically produce baby chicks and piglets. We'll also include some criteria for them to die if they are not provided with enough water and food.

So, our AI list for this game is as illustrated in the following table:

Gameobject	AI	Comments
Colt	N/A	Player controlled
Old farmer	N/A	Governed by dialog system
Baby chicks	Eat/drink Grow to Chicken Die	There will be multiple instances of this game object
Chicken	Eat/drink Create baby chicks Die	There will be multiple instances of this game object
Piglet	Eat/drink Grow to adult pig Die	There will be multiple instances of this game object

Gameobject	AI	Comments
Adult pig	Eat/drink

Create piglets

Die | There will be multiple instances of this game object |

End state

The final part of our game design is to determine how the game will end. There are two types of end states: victory and defeat. The victory condition is the end goal. This lets players know what they are working towards. We need to determine how players will beat the game. For Little Farmer Colt, we'll send the victory condition to the game state containing five full-grown chickens and five full-grown pigs. Full grown will be designated as blue ribbon animals. In a larger game, this end state might signify the ending of the first level. This gives you the opportunity to further develop the game when you are finished reading this book.

The other end state is defeat. We have already identified that the animals can die. So, we'll set the defeat condition to occur if there is not at least one of each type of animal. It will not matter whether the animals are chicks and piglets or chickens and pigs.

Okay, our game is fully designed. Now we can start creating our game environment. We'll start with terrain in the next section.

Terrain

Our game environment will be a rural farming setting with water and land features. We'll create our terrain with a water feature running down the middle of the land and a natural bridge that allows the player to travel between sides. On the left side of our terrain, we'll put Colt's farmhouse and areas for both chickens and pigs. The old farmer will have a farmhouse on the right side of the terrain, surrounded by a corn maze.

To make the land look a bit more interesting, we'll include some hills and trees. The following diagram shows a mockup up of what we'll create in the remainder of this chapter:

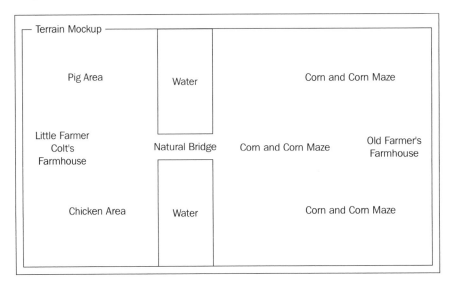

We'll create a Unity project and continually update it throughout the remainder of the book. To create the project, perform the following steps:

1. Launch the Unity application on your computer.
2. Click on the **New Project** button on initial Unity dialog window.
3. Enter LittleFarmerColt for the project name.
4. Select a folder location for your project. I recommend selecting an area that is automatically backed up by your system.
5. Ensure **3D** is selected.
6. Click on the **Create Project** button.

After you follow these steps, Unity will open your new project. In the next section, we'll start creating the terrain.

Creating the terrain

Unity treats terrain as a game object. You'll see reference to this in Unity as **GameObject**. Game objects are a fundamental feature in Unity. Everything is a game object, including characters, trees, lights, cameras, and more. These objects act as containers for components.

In Unity, projects contain game objects of all kinds. You'll be able to see all game objects in the **Project** view. You'll use some of these game objects in your scene. So, things (game objects) in a scene are visible in the **Hierarchy** view. When we drag game objects from the **Project** view into the **Hierarchy** view, we are creating an instance or copy of that game object.

You'll see later in the book how we can add components to game objects. For now, we want to create our game's terrain. We'll do this by performing the following steps:

1. In Unity, projects contain game objects of all kinds. You'll be able to see all game objects in the **Project** view. You'll use some of these game objects in your scene. So, things (game objects) in a scene are visible in the **Hierarchy** view. When we drag game objects from the **Project** view into the **Hierarchy** view, we are creating an instance or copy of that game object.

2. Select the **GameObject** drop-down menu, then select **3D Object**, and click on **Terrain**. This will create a terrain object. You'll see the object listed in **Hierarchy** and **Project** views:

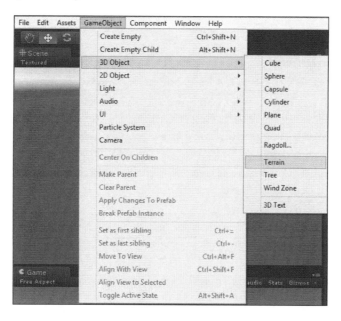

3. Next, we'll reduce the size of the terrain to something more manageable. We'll accomplish this by selecting **Terrain** in the **Hierarchy** view, and then selecting the **Terrain Settings** button ( ) in the **Inspector** view. Scroll down and change both the **Terrain Width** and **Terrain Length** to 250. This will result in the terrain being resized to 250x250.

> When we initially create a terrain in Unity, the origin of that terrain is in a corner. You can change the scene origin to (0,0,0) so that it is in the middle of the terrain. This can make it easier to manage the terrain.

4. Still in the **Inspector** view, click on the **Paint Height Tool** button ( ) and then click on the **Flatten** button. Note that when you "flatten" the terrain, the object may leave the frame in the **Scene** view. You can double-click on the object in the **Hierarchy** view to bring the object back in frame.

The terrain is created and we are now ready to add some features to our terrain.

Adding mountains

We'll create mountains and hills on our terrain to give it some character. Since our game is predominately a farm, we'll only put mountains around the edges of the terrain. This will help us keep things under control and prevent Colt, our game character, from falling off the edge of the earth.

Unity makes erecting mountains as simple as dragging your mouse's cursor. Here are the steps we'll use to create our mountains:

1. In the **Inspector** view, click on the **Raise/Lower Terrain** tool ( ).
2. You'll see a variety of brush types available to you in the **Inspector** view below the tool icons. Select one of the brush types with a single click. You can also change the brush size with the slider in the **Inspector** view or by entering in a numeric value.
3. Move your mouse over to the **Scene** view. When you push the left mouse button and drag the cursor over the terrain, you'll notice that you start painting mountains on the terrain.
4. Paint a row of mountains along all four edges of the terrain.

Our mountains and terrain do not look like much yet, so we'll get to that shortly.

Adding a river

Our next task is to create a river. You'll remember from our terrain mockup that we want the river to flow from one end of the terrain, down the middle to the opposite end. We'll tackle this task in two phases. The first phase is digging a trench, or lowering the terrain where we want the river. The second phase is adding the water. We'll take care of the first phase now. To do so, perform the following steps:

1. In the **Inspector** view, click on the **Raise/Lower Terrain** tool ( ).

2. Select a large brush size.

3. Move your mouse cursor into the **Scene** view.

4. Hold the *Shift* key down and keep the left mouse button pressed. Now, as you drag your mouse over the terrain, you'll be lowering the terrain.

5. Lower the terrain in the center, from one end of the terrain to the other. This will create an area for water that will effectively split the terrain in half visually.

6. If you did not leave an area for Colt to walk across the water, raise an area in the center now.

We will add water, the second phase of creating our river, later in this chapter.

Textures

Textures in Unity are image files that can be used for adding a textured surface to an object. At the onset, we do not have any textures loaded into Unity. We'll quickly add some terrain textures by performing the following steps:

1. Select the **Assets** drop-down menu, then select **Import Package**, and click on **Environment**, as shown in the following screenshot:

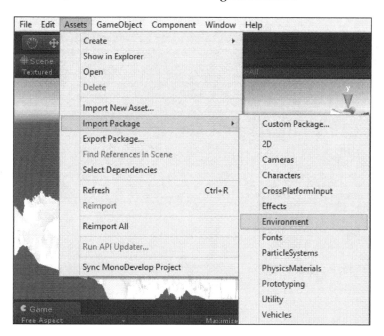

This will result in an **Import Package** dialog window popping up.

2. All the objects in the package will already be selected, so you simply need to click on the **Import** button to add this package to your Unity project. Click on the **Import** button.

This is a large package, so it might take a minute or more to import. We'll talk more about packages later in the book. For now, know that this is a quick way to add a lot of objects to your project.

Unity's **Environment** package came with several textures. If you expand the selections in the **Project** view, you'll notice that there is now a folder named **Standard Assets** or **SampleAssets**. The Environment package of assets is located in that folder. Within the **Environment** folder, you'll see a **Terrain** folder, as shown in the following screenshot:

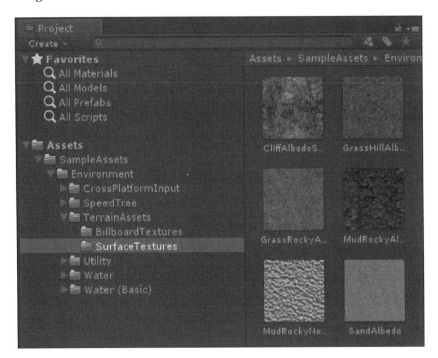

The **Terrain** folder contains, among other things, textures that we'll use to enhance our terrain. Let's do that now by performing the following steps:

1. Select **Terrain** in the **Hierarchy** view.

2. In the **Inspector** view, select the **Paint Texture** button ( ).

3. Still in the **Inspector** view, under the brushes section, you see an **Edit Textures** button to the far right. Click on that button:

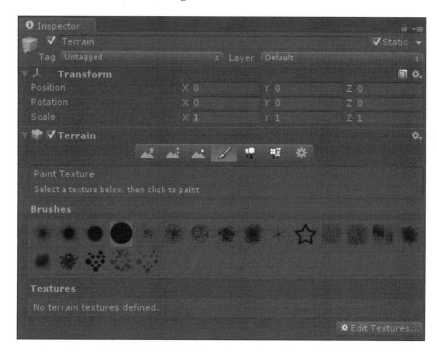

4. Clicking on the **Edit Textures** button results in a mini pop-up window. Select **Add Texture** from this menu.

5. In the **Add Terrain Texture** window, click on the **Select** button under **Texture**.

6. In the **Select Texture** window, scroll down until you see **MudRockyAlbedoSpecular** icon. Double-click on that icon.

7. Click on the **Add** button to add this texture to your terrain.

Your terrain should now have that texture applied to it and will look similar to the following screenshot:

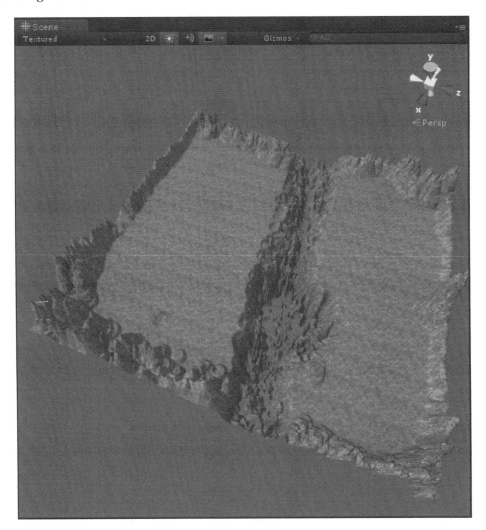

Our terrain looks a bit more realistic because we have applied a texture to it. Next, let's use a different texture to paint on the mountains. We'll accomplish that by performing the following steps:

1. Select **Terrain** in the **Hierarchy** view.

2. In the **Inspector** view, select the **Paint Texture** button.

3. Still in the **Inspector** view, under the brushes section, you will see the **Edit Textures** button to the far right. Click on that button.

4. Clicking on the **Edit Textures** button results in a mini pop-up window. Select **Add Texture** from this menu.

5. In the **Add Terrain Texture** window, click on the **Select** button under **Texture**.

6. In the **Select Texture** window, scroll down until you see **CliffAlbedoSpecular** icon. Double click on that icon.

7. Click on the **Add** button to add this texture to our available textures for painting.

8. Click on the new texture in the **Inspector** view.

9. Select a brush size that you are comfortable with.

10. Move your mouse cursor into the **Scene** view.

11. Hold down the left mouse button and move your cursor over the mountains. This will paint the next texture on the mountains.

Your terrain now has different textures for the ground and for the mountains, as shown in the following screenshot:

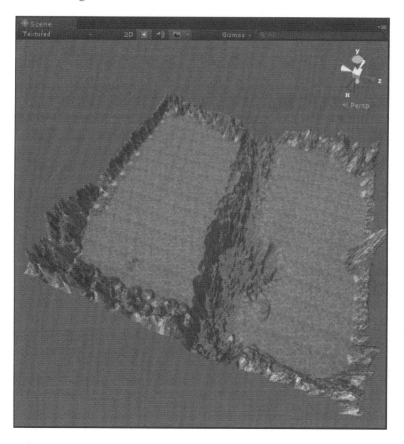

In the next section, we'll create the natural bridge, plant trees, add water, and create the sky.

Additional environmental features

We are now ready to enhance our terrain with additional features. First, we will add a natural bridge, and then we'll selectively plant trees. We'll also add water to the center of our terrain and create the sky.

Natural bridge

There are several ways to build a bridge for our game. We want the player to be able to walk from one side of the game map to the other. The approach we'll take is to use a textured geometric shape. Here are the steps:

1. Use the transform tools in the **Scene** view to zoom into the area you want to place the bridge. I will put it in the center of the terrain.

2. Select the **GameObject** drop-down menu, select the **3D Object**, and click on **Cube**.

3. Right-click on the cube in the **Hierarchy** view and select **Rename**. Rename the cube as `Bridge`.

4. Use the transform tool to increase the width and length of the cube. A scale of 12, 5, 58 works nicely.

5. Use the translate tool to move the bridge in place. Be sure to place both ends just beneath the surface so it does not look:

6. Right now, the bridge looks like a concrete slab. Let's apply a texture to it so it looks more natural. In the **Project** view, navigate to **Assets | SampleAssets | Environment | TerrainAssets | SurfaceTextures**, and then in the second column of the **Project** view, select the **GrassRockyAlbedo**. Drag this texture to the bridge in the **Hierarchy** view:

There we are, our bridge is in place and looks natural. Save your scene and your project.

Planting trees

Planting trees is easier in Unity than it is in real life. In fact, Unity gives us a few options. The option that gives us the most flexibility is to create our own tree from scratch. This is a bit time-consuming, but can result in highly unique trees.

We can also use pre-existing tree assets. There are some that are part of the **SampleAssets** that ship with Unity. And, as you would expect, there are several assets that are available from external sources. For our game, we'll use a tree that is readily available to us.

Before we start planting trees, we need to know where we want them. If you refer back to our terrain mockup, you'll see that we did not make any annotations for trees. Since our game involves farming, we do not have a great need for trees. We'll just plant a few for decorative purposes and to help make the game world seem more real.

We'll plant our trees by performing the following steps:

1. Use the transform tools in the **Scene** view to zoom out. You'll want to be able to see all or a large section of the terrain.

2. Select **Terrain** in the **Hierarchy** view.

3. In the **Inspector** view, click on the **Place Trees** () button.

4. Below this button, you'll see a **Trees** section and, beneath that, an **Edit Trees** button. Click on that button, as shown in the following screenshot:

5. When you click on the **Edit Trees** button, you'll be presented with a pop-up window. In that pop-up window, select **Add Tree**.

6. Click on the small circle to the right of the **Tree Prefab** line in the **Add Tree** dialog window. This will result in a **Select GameObject** dialog window.

7. In the **Select GameObject** dialog window, double-click on the **Conifer_Desktop** tree icon.

8. Click on the **Add** button in the **Add Tree** dialog window.

Now that we have added a tree to our terrain in the **Inspector** view, we can start placing them in our scene. First, we'll need to adjust some of our settings. We'll do this in the **Settings** section of the **Terrain** in **Inspector** view as shown in the following screenshot:

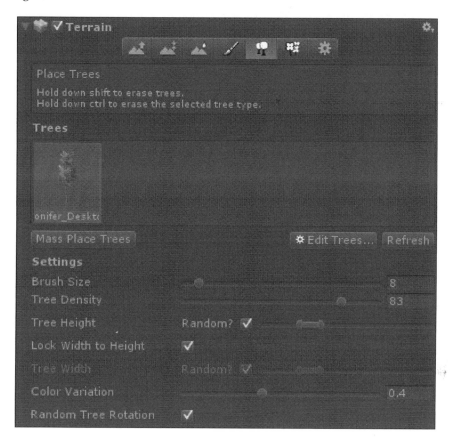

To add trees in our scene, perform the following steps:

1. Change the **Brush Size** to 8 and slightly reduce the **Tree Height** slider by moving it to the left.

2. Move your mouse into the **Scene** view and click on each spot you want to place a tree. You can use your mouse as a paintbrush to paint trees wherever you desire.

3. A quick method to get a lot of trees on your terrain is to use the **Mass Place Trees** button, which is just under the tree image in the **Inspector** view. When you click on this button, a **Place Trees** dialog window appears. Change the **Number Of Trees** field to 50 and click on the **Place** button, as shown in the following screenshot:

4. The function of randomly placing trees can be a big time saver. It can also place some trees where you do not want them. To erase trees, you simply select the **Place Trees** button in the **Inspector** view and shift-click on the trees in the **Scene** view. This erases any unwanted trees.

As you can see in the following image, I erased trees that were in the way of our farmland and in the river:

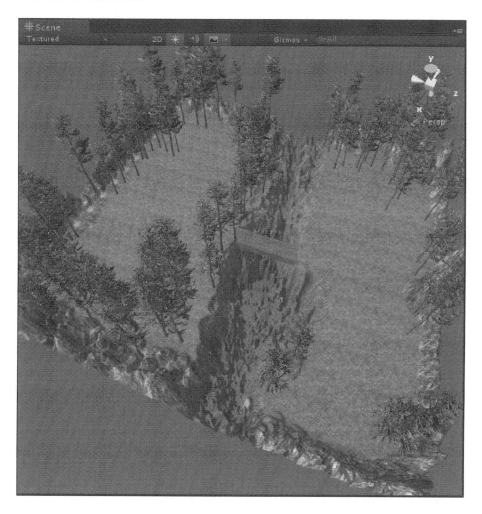

Water

We'll use a quick trick to add water to our terrain. Our approach will be to add a water object that comes standard with Unity and shape it in a manner that makes it look like a true body of water. To do so, perform the following steps:

1. In the **Project** view, navigate to **Assets | Sample Assets | Environment | Water (Basic) | Prefabs**. This will display two water objects in the second column of the **Project** view.

2. Click on the **WaterBasicDaytime** object in the second column of the **Project** view and drag it to the scene. You'll notice that the water is a flat, circle object.

3. Use the transform tools to change the size and location so that it covers the river and does not overflow on the bridge or land. Your terrain should now look similar to the following screenshot:

Creating the sky

The last enhancement we'll make to our terrain is to create a sky. We will use **Skybox**, which is a six-sided cube visible to the player beyond all other objects. Perform the following steps to create a Skybox:

1. Click on the **Assets** folder in the **Project** view.

2. Using the top menu bar, select **Assets** | **Create** | **Material**. This will create a new material object in the **Assets** folder.

3. Rename the new material as Skybox.

4. Select the Skybox asset in the **Project** view.

5. In the **Inspector** view, the **Shader** option is defaulted to **Standard**. Change that to Skybox/ 6 Sided. This will create six textural slots for your new material, as shown in the following screenshot:

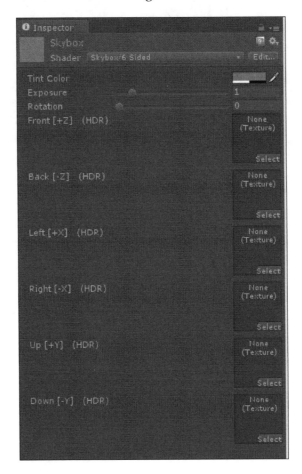

6. Drag the six image files from the Skybox set, which starts with the name CloudyLightRays into your Assets folder. You'll find these images in the folder 3852_02_SkyboxTextures, which is available with this book.

7. Drag each new file to the corresponding slot in the **Inspector** view. You'll notice that the files contain back, down, front, left, right, or up. Each of these has a corresponding slot in the Skybox. Once you finish this step, your **Inspector** view should present your Skybox, as shown in the following screenshot:

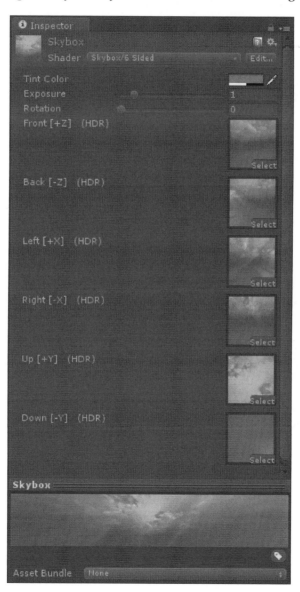

8. In the **Hierarchy** view, select the **Main Camera**.

9. Click on the **Add Component** button in the bottom of the **Inspector** view. Then, select **Rendering** and then **Skybox**. This will create new component in the **Inspector** view for your main camera:

10. Drag the **Skybox** asset we created into the **Custom Skybox** slot of the **Skybox** component in the **Inspector** view:

Now you can see in both the **Scene** view and **Game** view that the player has a 360 view of our Skybox.

Be sure to save your scene and your project.

Summary

In this chapter, we dabbled in the concept of game design and documented our Little Farmer Colt game. The game design will serve as a reference point for our remaining work on the game throughout this book. The game design also informed the characteristics of our terrain. We created a terrain, added a texture to the terrain, added mountains, trees, and a river. We even created a natural bridge. We concluded our chapter by adding a Skybox.

Our game's foundation is now created and you have the experience to create your own game environments.

In the next chapter, we'll take a close look at how to import and use assets in Unity. We'll do more than experiment; we'll actually import our game's main character Colt, the old farmer, and the animals.

3
Working with Assets

In the last chapter, we designed our game and created our game environment, the virtual world that our players will interact with during the game. Now, we are ready to start populating our game environment with more than just trees and water.

In this chapter, we will take a close look at importing Unity and third-party assets from Unity's Asset Store directly into our game. These assets will be used to make our game environment more enjoyable for users. We'll add our pig, piglet, baby chick, adult chicken, old farmer, and Colt, our young farmer. These are our game's characters.

We'll import barns for the two farmers. We'll also create our own 3D asset using free software and import it into our game.

After reading this chapter, you will:

- Understand what a Unity asset is
- Be able to import a Unity asset into your game
- Be able to import a third-party asset into your game
- Understand Unity packages
- Be able to import a Unity package into your game
- Be able to use Blender to export a 3D object
- Be able to import a 3D object made in Blender into your game

Assets

Assets are defined as useful or valuable things. In Unity, assets are useable game objects. There are three basic types of assets: Unity, user-created, and third party. As the names suggest, they are based on how the asset is created. Unity comes with free assets and offers a library of premium (not free) assets. User-created assets are those that you create yourself. We will create our own assets later in this chapter. The final asset type is third party, which indicates that someone other than you or Unity created it.

When we select the **Assets** drop-down menu, we see several functions available to us. The functions we'll cover in this chapter are **Create**, **Import New Asset...**, and **Import Package**, as shown in the following screenshot:

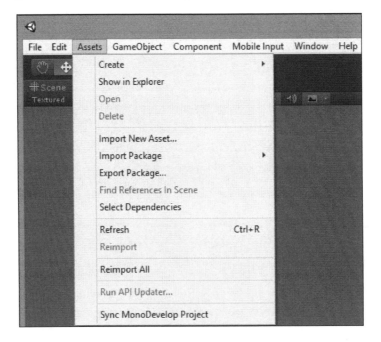

Navigating to **Assets | Create** reveals several types of assets we can create directly from within Unity. You'll notice that assets can be scripts, shaders, prefabs, materials, animations, and more. Assets are essentially any item we use in our game. We'll use some of these in later chapters as we complete our game.

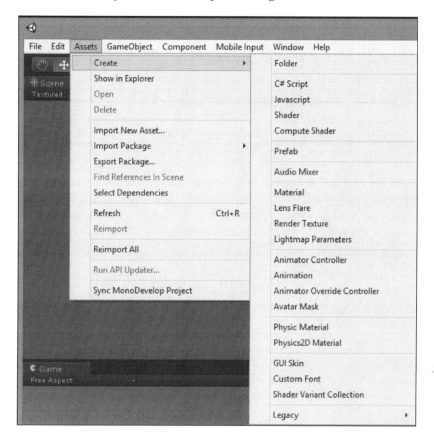

We can also create basic 3D assets, such as a cube and a sphere. To create a physical 3D object, you would navigate to **GameObject | 3D Object**, as shown in the following screenshot, and select what object to create. Using these objects may not be what you need for your game, and we certainly do not need them for *Little Farmer Colt*. These assets are great for testing components and scripts in Unity projects. We can delete them that than we can create them, so they make great and expendable test assets. These objects are great for prototyping. We can use them in our games to experiment before we spend any time on final graphics.

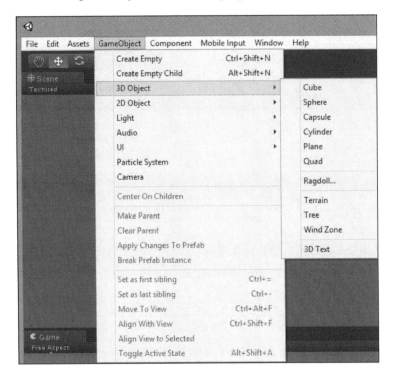

Asset packages

In the last chapter, we imported an asset package so that we could create and modify our game's terrain. In this section, we'll look at what these packages are and how we'll use them in Unity and for our game.

Asset packages are bundles of assets grouped together. We can create packages to share our assets with others or to save them for use in another game or Unity application. We can even create asset bundles to sell in Unity's Asset Store.

To create an asset package, you simply select all the assets you want in the package, using the **Project** view. Then you have two options. Your first option is to right-click and select **Export Package**. The second option is to navigate to **Assets | Export Package**. Both options result in the same outcome.

In addition to the ability to export packages from Unity, we can also import asset packages into Unity. To import an asset package, we simply navigate to **Assets | Import Package** menu option:

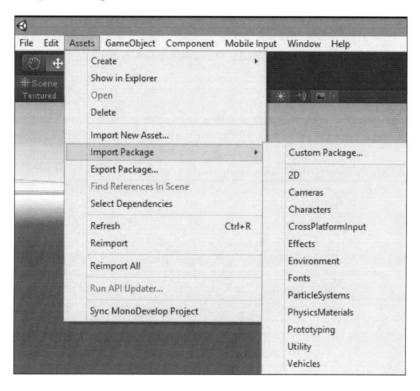

When importing asset packages, we can select from one of the 12 asset packages that ship from Unity. These packages are listed when the **Assets | Import Package** menu is selected, as shown in the following screenshot. Selecting one of these packages to import results in Unity decompressing the package, then displaying the package contents to you:

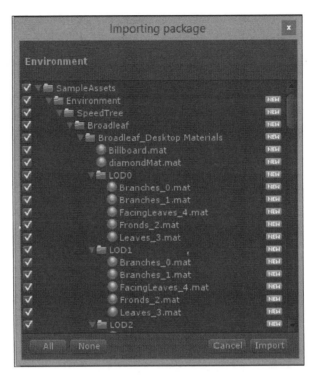

After the package has been decompressed and before the assets in that package are imported into your Unity project, you have the opportunity to review, select, and deselect assets in the package. Once you have the desired packages selected, you simply click on the **Import** button. Unity will place the package in your project. You'll be able to see the assets in **Project** view.

The actual files are stored in your project's folder hierarchy in the same file/folder structure you saw when you reviewed the assets prior to importing them. This makes things easy to find.

 Be sure not to move assets using your computer's file and folder system. Relocating assets outside of Unity can result in linkage problems for your project. You can move things around from within Unity in the **Project** view with no consequences.

We also have the option to import a **Custom Package** option by navigating to **Assets | Import Package** menu selection. When this option is selected, you'll be presented with a dialog window so you can indicate where on your computer the package is. The file extension for Unity packages is `.unitypackage`.

Unity Asset Store

Unity operates a store called the Unity Asset Store. There are a great number of assets available to Unity developers. The store is accessible directly on the Web at `http://assetstore.unity3d.com`. You can also open a window within Unity to display the Asset Store. This is accomplished by navigating to **Window | Asset Store**.

Regardless of how you connect to the Unity Asset Store, you'll see a hierarchical category listing in the top-right corner of the store:

Clicking on the triangular icons to the left of each category reveals subcategories. Some categories have multiple subcategories, which helps you find what you are looking for quickly.

When you click on a category, its contents will be viewable. Clicking on a specific asset will display several characteristics of that asset. These characteristics include:

- Title
- Publisher
- Rating

- Price
- Purchase button or, in the case of free assets, an "Open in Unity" button
- Version of Unity required
- Description
- Package contents
- File size
- Version number (of the asset)
- Images
- Videos (not always available)
- Link to publisher's website

There are a couple of things to consider regarding obtaining assets from the Unity Asset Store. First, you'll want to make sure that you have the requisite rights to use the asset as you plan to. For example, if you do not have commercial use rights, you will not want to use that particular asset in your commercial game.

Another thing to consider before selecting assets from the Asset Store is how large the files are. Fortunately, this information is part of the metadata displayed when you preview an asset.

In the next section, we'll visit the Unity Asset Store, select an asset, and add that asset to our game project.

Adding assets to your game

Let's add some assets to our *Little Farmer Colt* game. First, we'll visit the Unity Asset Store, select an asset, inspect it, download it, and add it to our game. Next, we'll import a custom asset package.

Using the Unity Asset Store

The following steps illustrate how to find an asset from the Unity Asset Store and add it to our game. We'll look at specific characteristics of the asset, so you know what to look at when using the store.

1. Launch Unity and open your project. Remember, we named our project `LittleFarmerColt`.

2. Open your scene by navigating to **File | Open Scene** menu selection. This will bring up a **Load Scene** file dialog box with your project's `Assets` folder displayed. The name of my scene is **FarmScene**. Double-click on the scene file to open it. Alternatively, single-click on the scene file and click on the **Open** button, as shown in the following screenshot:

Now we are ready to open the Unity Asset Store. We will search for an object appropriate for our game.

3. From the drop-down menus, navigate to **Window | Asset Store**. This will open the Asset Store in a new window.

4. If you are not already logged in with your Unity account, log in now. You'll see a **Log In** link in the top-right corner of the window. You should have created an account when you downloaded Unity. If not, use the **Create Account** link, as shown in the following screenshot:

5. Once you are logged in, you'll see your name in the top-right corner of the store's window, replacing the **Create Account** and **Log In** links, as shown in the following screenshot:

6. Using the search box just below your username, type `pickaxe` and hit the *Return* key:

7. You'll see several assets returned in your search. Scroll through the search results until you find the pickaxe asset from Unity Technologies, as shown in the following screenshot:

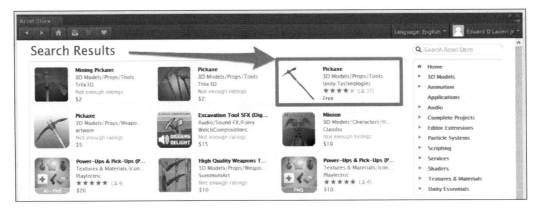

Because the Unity Asset Store is continuously updated, it is possible that the pickaxe from Unity Technologies might not be available. If this is the case, browse through the assets and select one that is free and, preferably, from Unity Technologies.

8. Click on the pickaxe image icon to bring up details on that asset.

We are presented with several key pieces of information about the asset. The title and image preview are the most notable. In the top left area, we see the category and sub-categories the asset belongs to, the publisher, rating, and price. Below that section is a **Download** button.

Just below the **Download** button, there is a brief description of the asset and copyright information. This area's content will differ, based on the asset that you are viewing.

In addition to asset changes in the Asset Store, the layout and search functionality is subject to change. So, if you see something different to the screenshots presented in this chapter, do not be alarmed.

The next section of the asset preview shows the version number, file size, and a link to the publisher's website. If you have questions about the asset or problems with it after you download it, you can use the link shown in the following screenshot to contact the publisher:

Version: 1.0 (Jun 03, 2011)   Size: 138.8 kB   Visit Publisher's Website

The final section of the asset preview is the **Package Contents** area. Here you'll see a hierarchical list of all elements of the package. Remember, an asset package is a collection of assets.

The pickaxe package contains four items. It contains a text file with licensing information, a material file, the pickaxe object, and a .png file. Some assets can be previewed in the editor. Try clicking on the .mat file to see the preview. The preview is shown in the following screenshot:

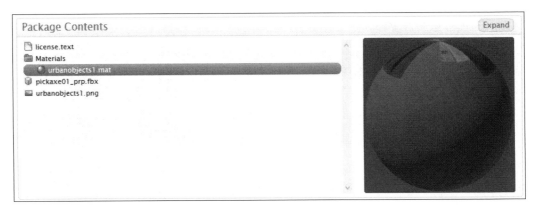

1. Click on the **Download** button in the Unity Asset Store window. This will bring up an **Importing Package** dialog window. Depending on your Internet connection, this could take anywhere from a few moments to several minutes. All assets in the package are selected by default. If you do not want specific components of the package, you can deselect them here.

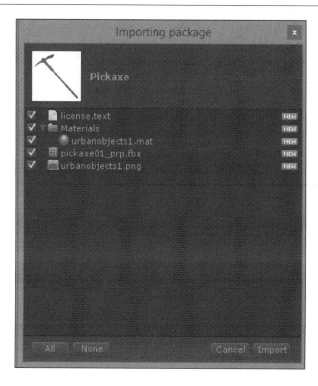

2. Click on the **Import** button.

3. In the **Project** view, right-click on the top **Assets** folder and navigate to **Assets | Create | Folder** menu choice. Name the folder `pickaxe`.

4. In the **Project** view, drag the components of the pickaxe package into the pickaxe folder you just created. Once you have completed this, your **Project** view should look similar to the following screenshot:

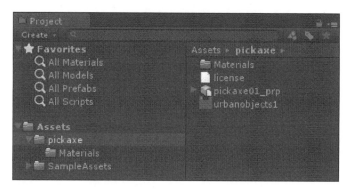

5. Close the Unity Asset Store window.

Now you have the pickaxe asset available to you for the game. For now, we'll leave it in the **Project** view.

Importing a custom asset package

We are now ready to upload our game characters and buildings. There are two asset packages on the book's web page. The first package, character_assets. unitypackage, contains the two farmers, piglet, pig, baby chick, and chick. The second package, building_assets.unitypackage, contains the two barns, one for each famer. We'll upload them individually.

Importing the game characters

Perform the following steps to load the game characters into your game:

1. Download the character_assets.unitypackage from this book's web page.

2. Launch Unity and open your project.

3. From the top drop-down menu, navigate to **Assets | Import Package | Custom Package**. This will display the **Import Package** dialog window.

4. In the **Import Package** dialog window, navigate to where you saved the character assets file. Select that file.

5. Click on the **Open** button.

6. Unity will automatically decompress the package and then display the **Importing Package** dialog window. All of the assets will already be selected. Click on the **Import** button. You will see a **Hold On** progress window that displays each component as it is imported. Once the import is completed, you'll see several new objects in the **Project** view.

You can see that there are now chick, chicken, farmer, farmer boy, pig adult, and piglet assets. We'll work with these in later chapters.

Save your project.

Importing the buildings

Perform the following steps to load the buildings into your game:

1. Download the `building_assets.unitypackage` from this book's web page.
2. Launch Unity and open your project.
3. From the top drop-down menu, navigate to **Assets** | **Import Package** | **Custom Package.** This will display the **Import Package** dialog window.
4. In the **Import Package** dialog window, navigate to where you saved the building assets file. Select that file.
5. Click on the **Open** button.
6. Unity will automatically decompress the package and then display the **Importing Package** dialog window. All of the assets will already be selected. Click on the **Import** button. You will see a **Hold On** progress window that displays each component as it is imported. Once the import is completed, you'll see that the **barn1** and **barn2** assets are now available in the **Project** view.
7. Save your project.

Using Blender to create assets for your game

We previously discussed the ability for us to create assets outside of Unity, export them into a format compatible with Unity, and then import them into our game. In this section, we'll do just that.

There are several tools that can be used to create 3D objects for use in Unity. One of the most commonly used is Blender. Blender is a free and open source 3D modeling program that has an impressive array of capabilities. There are several books and online tutorials that can teach you how to use Blender to create assets. Teaching you how to create them from scratch is beyond the scope of this book.

What we do have time to discuss is how to take a Blender object and export it into a Unity-supported format. Let's do that together by performing the following steps:

1. If you do not already have a copy of Blender on your computer, download a copy from `http://www.blender.org`.
2. Download the `corn_stalk.blend` file from this book's web page.

3. Launch Blender.

4. In Blender, navigate to **File | Open** to open a file dialog window.

5. Navigate to the `corn_stalk.blend` file you previously downloaded. Select the file.

6. Click on the **Open Blender File** button, which is located in the top-right corner of the window. You'll now be able to see the object in Blender.

Take a look at the following screenshot:

The preceding screenshot shows how the object looks after it has been created in Blender. Now, we simply need to export it so we can use it in Unity. To do so, perform the following steps:

1. Navigate and select **File | Export | FBX (.fbx)** to export the object to an `.fbx` file.

2. Select a file location for the file.

3. Click on the **Export FBX** button located in the top-right corner of the window.

4. Launch Unity and open your project.

5. Navigate and select **Assets | Import New Asset** from the drop-down menu. This brings up the **Import New Asset** dialog window.

6. Navigate to where you saved the `.fbx` file. Select the file and click on the **Import** button.

7. Close Blender.

8. Save your Unity project.

You'll now see the corn stalk asset listed in the **Project** view.

Summary

In this chapter, we covered Unity assets and asset packages. You visited the Unity Asset Store and reviewed what information is available on assets located in the Store. You gained experience downloading and importing assets into your game. You also learned a little about how to create 3D objects using Blender, a free and open-source 3D modeling tool.

In the next chapter, you'll animate the game's characters. The animations will include idle animations for all characters, both human and animal, talk animations for the farmers. Colt, our player-controlled character, will also receive walk and take animations. The take animation will be for the harvesting of corn and water. And, just for fun, we'll give Colt the ability to jump.

4
Animating the Game Characters

So far, our game's design is complete, our game environment has been created, and we have imported game characters and other assets into our game. The game characters we added were the pig, piglet, baby chick, adult chicken, old farmer, and Colt, our young farmer. Our game characters would be boring if they just stood there like a rock. We'll breathe life into our characters and game by adding animations to each of the characters.

We will give each animal two animations so they can have some movement when they are idle, as well as when they eat. The old farmer will have talk and idle animations. The young farmer is our player-controlled character, so he will be able to walk, talk, run, take, and be idle.

After reading this chapter, you will:

- Understand what Unity animations are
- Understand what a player controller is
- Be able to preview animations
- Be able to animate the game's characters
- Be able to create an animation clip

Animation basics

Animation is defined as a simulated movement, which is created by displaying a series of pictures or frames. In Unity, animations are displayed similar to the method used in movies, which involves displaying of a specific number of progressive frames each second. We use animations to bring our characters to life.

When a player uses arrow keys or another input device to move the game's main character around the screen, it is being animated. So, the game is responding to the user's input and playing the appropriate animation. For example, when the player holds the left arrow key down, the game's main character walks to the left. This is a walking animation in Unity.

Animations are typically created by using a 3D modeling tool such as Blender, 3D Studio Max, or Maya. As you will see later in this chapter, we can also create animations from within Unity.

For our game, we have two primary concerns regarding animation. First, we want to animate the young famer character so that the user can control where he goes and what he does. The first thing we need to do is to create a character controller.

Character controllers

There are two types of player characters in games: those controlled by human players and those controlled by computers. The first type is known as a player character while the other type is referred to as a non-player character. Player characters can be almost anything you can imagine. In modern games, player characters are usually human or humanoid. This is not to say you cannot create a game in which the player character is an uprooted tree or a rock with seven legs. For our game, the player character will be a human boy named Colt.

Unity uses a game object called a character controller to enable user controls. There are two types of character controllers in Unity. The two types are first person controller and third person controller. The types refer to the user perspective, first or third, used during the game. Take a look at the following image that shows the player perspective:

Player Perspectives

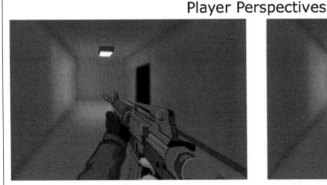 

First Person　　　　　　　Third Person

With first person controllers, only part of the player's character is visible on screen. Most games will display hands, arms, fists, weapons, or some combination. The perspective the game is played is essentially through the character's eyes. Third person controllers allow the entire character to be seen during gameplay.

First person controller

We will not need a first person controller in our *Little Farmer Colt* game, but it is important to understand how to create one for other games you might create with Unity.

 This section provides instructions based on the assumption that you have worked through the previous chapters. If you get stuck on a step, refer back to the earlier chapter that covers that step.

To create a first person controller, perform the following steps:

1. Launch Unity.
2. Create a new 3D project.
3. Import the **Characters and Environment Asset Packages**.
4. Create a new terrain and add a texture to it. This will help you see the first person controller object in the **Scene** view.
5. In the **Project** view, navigate and select **Assets | Sample Assets | Characters | FirstPersonCharacter | Prefabs**.
6. In the **Project** view's second column, select the **FPSController** object and drag it to the **Scene** view. Release the mouse and you will have a first person controller in your scene:

A cylinder shape represents the first person controller. The controller can be tied to an avatar so that it looks like an actual character. Because this is a first person controller, you will not see any part of the character when you put your game in play mode.

Click on the **play** button to test the controller in game play mode. You can move the controller around with the arrow keys.

There is a lot more to the first person controller. If you intend to create a game that uses this controller, you'll gain great insights in Unity's online documentation. For more complex games, developers typically create custom controllers.

Creating a third person controller

Unity comes with a third person controller asset as part of the character package. The avatar associated with this controller is called Ethan.

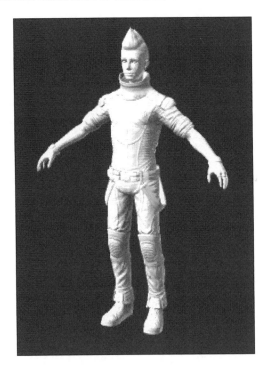

This is a great avatar to experiment with, but there is no place for Ethan in our game. To allow players to control the little farmer character, we'll need to implement a third person controller for him instead of Ethan. To do so, perform the following steps:

1. Launch Unity.

2. Open the game project.

3. Load the scene.

4. Using the transform tools in **Scene** view, adjust the view of the terrain so we are looking at the bridge from ground level. This will help you see where to place the character.

5. In the **Project** view, select the **SampleAssets** folder.

6. From the top menu, navigate and select **Assets | Import Package | Characters**. The asset package will be decompressed and then the **Importing package** dialog window will be displayed. Ensure all items are checked and then click on the **Import** button.

7. In the **Project** view, expand the folders until you see **SampleAssets | Characters | ThirdPersonCharacter | Prefabs**. Click on the **Prefabs** folder. In the **Project** view's second column, you will see an object labeled **ThirdPersonController**.

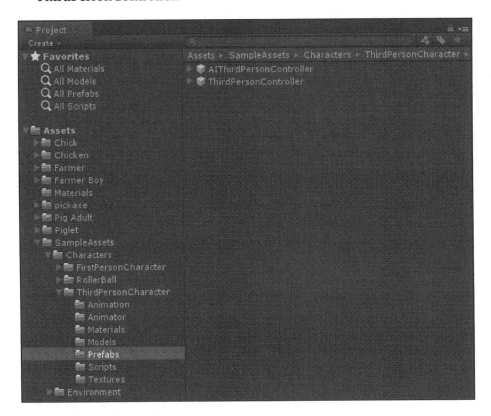

8. Click on the **ThirdPersonCharacter** object and drag it into the **Scene** view. Drop the object on top of the bridge.

9. Zoom in on the new object and you will see that it is Ethan encased in a character controller.

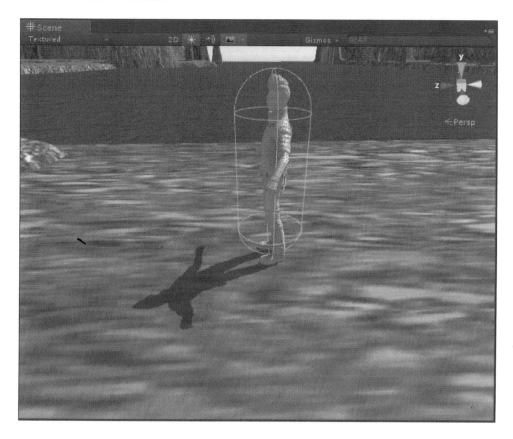

At this point, you can run the game in play mode and use Ethan to explore the game environment. Next, we'll swap out Ethan for Colt. To do so, perform the following steps:

1. In the **Scene** view, expand the **ThirdPersonController** object. You will see three items listed, all starting with the name Ethan:

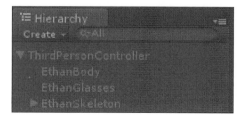

2. Delete the three items that start with the name Ethan. At this point, our third person controller still exists; it is just lacking an avatar.

3. In **Project** view, navigate and select **Assets | Farmer Boy** and then, in the second column, select the **FarmerBoy** object.

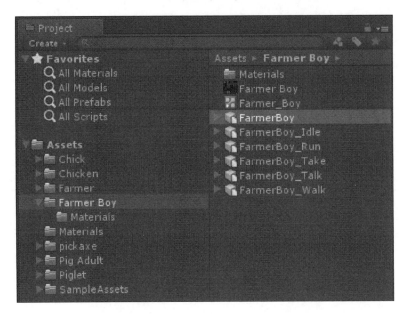

4. Drag the **FarmerBoy** object from the **Project** view to the **Hierarchy** view and drop it on top of the **ThirdPersonController** object:

5. You will now see Colt standing on the bridge, instead of Ethan.

6. Save the scene and the project. You should do this often.

7. The next thing we need to do is to tell Unity which controller to use for the Animator. In the **Hierarchy** view, navigate and select **ThirdPersonController | FarmerBoy**.

8. In the **Inspector** view, select the small circle icon to the right of the **Controller** text box. This is in the **Animator** section of the **Inspector** view.

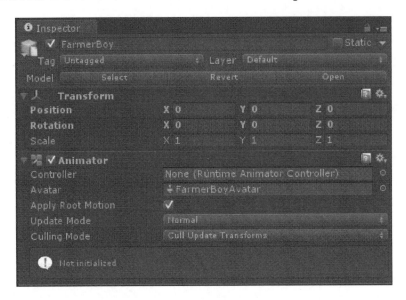

9. The **Select RuntimeAnimatorController** window will appear. Click on the **Assets** tab and then double-click on the **Farmer_Boy** item:

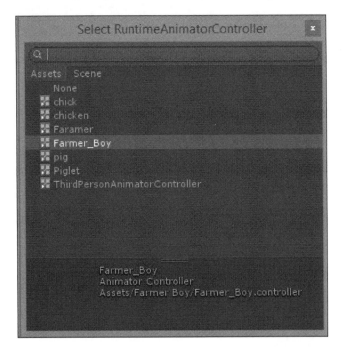

10. Select the third person controller that was chosen in the **Hierarchy** view.

11. In the **Inspector** view, you will notice that we have Ethan as our avatar. Although we have already changed this, changing the **Runtime Animation Controller** option has changed the setting:

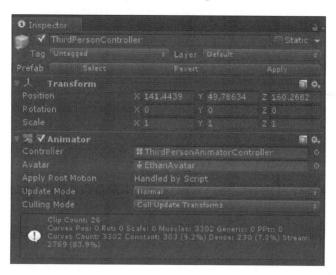

12. So, if you see Ethan listed as the avatar in the **Animator** section of the **Inspector** view, click on the little circle to the right of that field and select **FarmerBoyAvatar** from the **Select Avatar** dialog window.

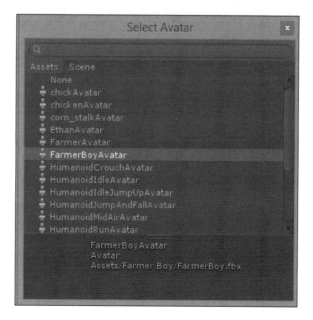

13. In the **Scene** view, zoom in on the character so you can see the player controller. Remember, a light green-framed cylinder represents the player controller. You'll notice that the cylinder is smaller than Colt. We must make sure that our character fits inside the character controller.

14. Select the **ThirdPersonController** option in the **Hierarchy** view. With this selected, we will make changes to the **Capsule Collider** section of the **Inspector** view.

15. In the **Inspector** view, in the **Capsule Collider** section, change the **Center Y** value to 0.8, the **Radius** value to 1, and the **Height** value to 6.

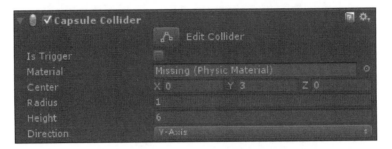

16. The **Capsule Collider** should now completely encapsulate Colt. Zoom in on Colt in the **Scene** view to make sure your collider is large enough.

17. We need to make one final change. We'll change Colt's y coordinate so that he is slightly above the ground. In the **Inspector** view, change the **Position Y Transform** value to 0.2. This will prevent Colt from falling through the terrain.

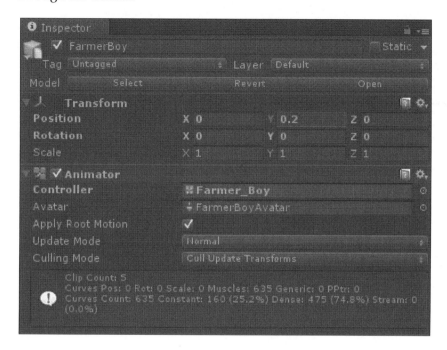

You can now put your game into play mode and watch the Colt character come to life. You can use the arrow keys to rotate him and to have him explore the game world.

 One word of caution: Colt cannot swim, nor can he walk on water. So, at least for now, I recommend keeping him out of the water.

In later sections, we'll add more animations and functionality to Colt.

Animating player characters

Our game, like most games, will consist of animated characters. Even if a non-player character only has a looped idle animation, it is important that they be animated. Otherwise, the characters will be more of a statue than a character.

Little farmer Colt

Let's continue working on our Colt character and ensure all of his animations work. By browsing the assets in the **Project** view, you can see there are five animations associated with Colt. The animations are idle, run, take, talk, and walk. These animations have already been created, so we are able to use them in our game.

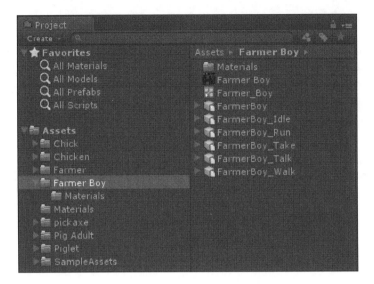

Some of the animations will simply just seem to work because of the character controller we used. For example, if you test the game in play mode, you'll see that our walk animation is responsive to the navigation keys on our keyboard as well as the WASD keys. Also, although we did not create a jump animation, Colt already knows how to jump. You can test this by pressing the space bar while in game mode.

This is not magic; rather, it is a benefit of using the Unity game engine's third person character controller. Some animations will be part of the character by default, others we will create in external tools, and some we will create within Unity.

Old farmer character

We can add the old farmer character to our game by simply dragging the object from **Project** view into **Scene** view. We are not ready to do that just yet, but we do want to review his animations. By navigating through the **Project** view assets, you will notice that the old farmer has idle, talk, and walk animations. Although we will not use the walk animation for our game, it is included so you can expand the game after you finish working through the instructions provided in this book.

Farm animals

Browsing the remaining assets reveals that the chick, chicken, pig adult, and piglet each have an idle and eat animation. There is nothing more for these animals to do than stand around and eat. As you'll see later in this book, we will add scripts to the animals so that we know how much they eat and grow.

Previewing animations

When our game is being played, the characters will all have idle animations that play when the character is idle. The eat animations will be played when there is food to eat or water to drink. Colt's walk animation will be played in response to keyboard or mouse input. We'll add scripts that handle Colt's "take" animation, as well as the talk animations for the two farmers.

Unity provides us with the ability to preview animations without having to complete the game first and add our scripts. Our game has 16 animations, so being able to preview them without programming them into our game is a great time saver.

Let's preview Colt's animations. The steps are the same for all animations. In the following steps, we'll focus on the take animation:

1. In the **Project** view, navigate and select **Assets | Farmer Boy | FarmerBoy_Take**.

2. In the **Inspector** view, click on the **Animations** tab, as shown in the following screenshot:

3. In the **Inspector** view, click and drag the expand section bar upward so that the window with Colt in is large enough to view, as shown in the following screenshot:

4. With the preview window large enough to view, click on the **play** button in the top-left corner of the preview window. You will now see the animation play.

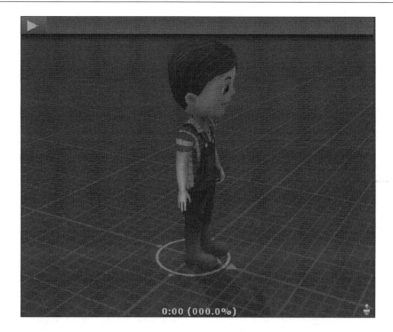

Now that you know how to preview animations in the game project, you should check the remaining 15 animations so you know how they work. In the next section, we will create our own animation by using Unity's built-in animation clip creation functionality.

Creating animation clips

Animation clips are small animation sequences in Unity. They can be very small, isolated pieces of motion. For example, walking is a valid animation. Associated animation clips will be walk right, walk left, look up, look down, bounce, and more. Multiple animation clips can make up a single animation.

Unity has internal capabilities to create custom animation clips. This represents a great and relatively quick way of building an animation clip. Perform the following steps to create a short animation clip for our Colt character:

1. Launch Unity.
2. Open the *Little Farmer Colt* project and scene.
3. In **Hierarchy** view, select the **ThirdPersonController** object.

4. In the **Scene** view, zoom in as necessary so that you can clearly see the Colt character.

5. Using the drop-down menu, navigate and select **Window | Animation**. This will bring up the **Animation** window. You'll see that the Colt character has a lot of animation clips listed in the window.

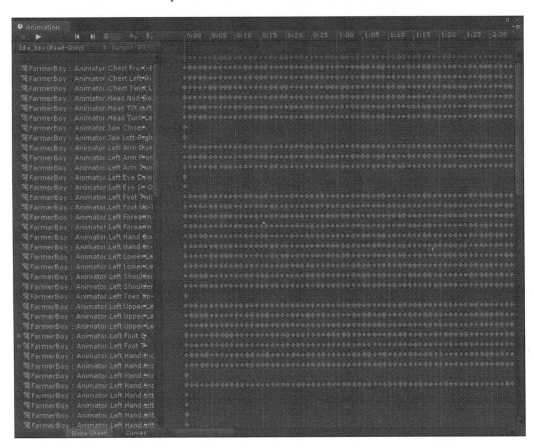

You'll notice in the top-left section of the **Animation** window, there are play controls and just beneath them, the Idle_boy animation is selected. If you were to click on the play button in the top-left corner of the **Animation** window, you would see the Idle_boy animation clip play in the **Scene** view. This is another method of previewing animation clips.

Now, perform the following steps:

1. In the **Animation** window, click on the up/down (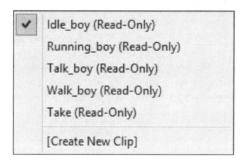) button to the right of the **Idle_boy (Read-Only)** text. This will bring up a list of animations for the current character, as shown in the following screenshot:

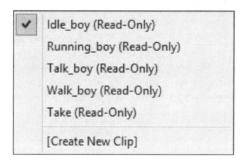

2. At the bottom of the current pop-up dialog, select **[Create New Clip]**. This will bring up a **Create New Animation** dialog window. The dialog window prompts you for a name of the new animation and a place to store it. Name the animation `Wave_boy`, accept all other defaults, and click on the **Save** button.

3. The **Animation** window now has the `Wave_boy` animation selected and no animation clips are associated with it yet:

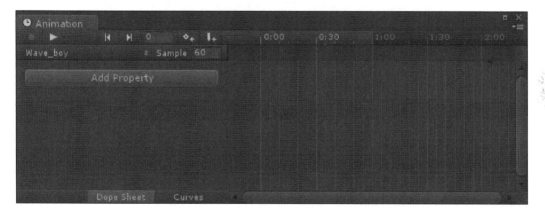

4. If necessary, move the **Animation** window so that it does not obstruct your view of the **Scene** view.

5. Click on the record () button. Once this button is clicked, you are ready to start recording the new animation. You'll notice that the record button is now highlighted in red and there is a vertical red line in the timeline portion of the **Animation** window.

6. Click on the **Add Property** button in the **Animation** window.

7. Expand the **Transform** section of the pop-up dialog window, as shown in the following screenshot:

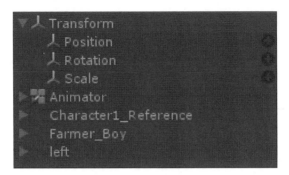

8. Click on the plus symbol () to the right of **Transform | Position**. This adds a starting position to our animation. If the character is not standing on the ground, use the transform tools as needed.

9. We have a starting position, now we'll advance the timeline to the 2-second mark. To do this, drag the vertical red line in the timeline to the right.

> If you do not see enough granularity in the timeline, you can expand the Animation window.

An alternative method to adjusting the timeline is to type the desired position directly into the frames text box:

10. In the **Animation** window, navigate and select **Transform | Rotation** and then click on the plus icon. This adds another action to the animation.

11. In **Scene** view, slightly rotate the character to the right.

12. Move the timeline to the 4-second mark.

13. Click on the **Add Property** button in the **Animation** window.

14. Navigate and select **Character1_Reference | Transform | Rotation** and then click on the plus icon.

15. In **Scene** view, slightly rotate the character to the left.

16. In the **Animation** window, click on the play button to test the animation. It might not look much like a wave, but the character does move back and forth. This is a great start to a wave animation.

17. Click on the **record** button to stop the recording.

18. Close the **Animation** window.

19. You'll now see the animation clip listed in **Project** view.

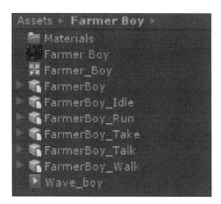

Summary

In this chapter, you learned how to add life to your game with the use of animations. You gained experience with first and third person controllers and learned about game player perspectives. This chapter guided you through the process of customizing the third person controller so our game would feature our little farmer character. You previewed animations and even created your own custom animation.

In the next chapter, you will be introduced to scripting with Unity. You'll learn how to use a tool called **MonoDevelop** and how to access your game's scripts. Specifically, we'll script our game so that, by the end of the chapter, you will be able to play a working version.

5
Scripting the Game

Our game is really taking shape. So far, we've completed the game design, game environment, player character, non-player characters, and animations. That is a lot of work for just four chapters. There are a few things we need to accomplish in order to complete our game. First on this list is scripting the game.

In this chapter, we will write scripts for:

- Managing the amount of water and corn that Colt collects
- Monitoring how much water and corn each farm animal is given
- Managing when a piglet becomes a pig and when a baby chick becomes an adult chicken
- Managing when pigs and chickens reach blue ribbon status

Before we dive right into scripting, I'll provide a C# programming primer for those that need it. We'll also review how scripting is accomplished in Unity, where to find scripts, and how to use MonoDevelop.

After reading this chapter, you will:

- Understand the fundamentals of C#
- Be able to use MonoDevelop to create and edit scripts
- Be able to locate scripts in a Unity project
- Understand how to read Unity scripts
- Be able to create custom scripts

 Throughout this chapter, you will see the terms scripting and programming used interchangeably. In the context of this chapter, they are the same thing.

C# programming primer

C# is a comprehensive programming language. Teaching you how to use this language is beyond the scope of this book. I'll provide enough information in this section so that you can understand the custom scripts we'll be writing for our game.

 For a deeper understanding of how to program using the C# language, you can use one of the many books available from Packt Publishing on the subject.

C# is both a function-based and object-oriented language. Functions are reusable sections of code that we script. For example, if we create a script called *feedPig*, it might handle transferring water and corn from Colt to a pig. Since we have multiple pigs in our game, this function would probably get used a lot.

As I've mentioned, C# is also an **object-oriented programming (OOP)** language. OOP languages use classes, which are sets of data and functions. If we have a `babyChick` class, for example, that class can hold data on how much corn the baby chick has eaten. That same class can perform the operation of growing the chick into an adult chicken.

Syntax

Programming language syntax is similar to written sentence structure and grammar. When we program in any language, we must be aware of how to structure our syntax. To illustrate these points, let's consider the following line of C# code:

```
int cornAmount = 0;
```

The following is a list of what that line of code is about:

- On the left side of the equals sign is `int cornAmount`. A new variable (`cornAmount`) is being declared as an integer. So, `int` followed by a variable name is how we declare an integer.
- The `= 0` attribute assigns a value to the integer. In this case, the value is zero.
- The end of the line of code is signified by the semicolon (`;`)

The following are a few tips to remember regarding programming in C#:

- Spaces do not generally matter unless they are part of a string. For the most part, extra spaces are simply ignored by C#.
- Case (uppercase and lowercase) makes a difference. For example, `cornAmount` and `cornamount` are not the same.

Naming conventions

It is helpful to use a naming convention system when programming. There are a couple of reasons for doing this. First, it makes the code easier to read. It also makes it easier for people other than the original programmer to quickly understand the code. A third benefit of using a naming convention is so that you can program faster.

The following are some examples of standard naming conventions.

Class, function, and method names

Names of classes, functions, and methods should have the first letter of each word capitalized. In the following example, EatCorn, Start, and Update follow this convention:

```
public class EatCorn : MonoBehavior {

  void Start ( ) {
  }

  void Update ( ) {
  }
}
```

Camel case

Variables and arguments use the convention known as camelCase where the first word is lower case and each subsequent word starts with an uppercase letter. The following are three examples:

pigletGrowth

coltCornHolding

chickenEatCorn

Abbreviations

Abbreviations should be avoided when programming, with a few exceptions. You've already seen me use int for integer. In addition to this being an abbreviation, it is a key word in C#. The following are some examples that show when not to use abbreviations:

Bad Example	Good Example
p1CrnCon	piglet1CornConsumed
cknay	chickenArray

Bad Example	Good Example
plyH20Hld	playerWaterHeld

The point of this convention is to make the scripts more readable.

Special characters

Special characters such as dashes and underscores should generally be avoided. They can increase the number of possible mistakes that could be made when scripting. So, use `chickenArray` instead of `chicken_Array`. Of course, if you are comfortable using dashes and underscores, I recommend that you maintain consistency in their use.

Data types

There are over a dozen types of data used in the C# programming language and you can even create your own. The following are the ones we'll use in our *Little Farmer Colt* game:

Data Type	Description
Boolean (bool)	True or False
Integer (int)	Whole number between -2,147,483,648 and 2,147,483,647
String (string)	String values such as "*Hello Farmer Colt*"
Array	You can think of arrays as spreadsheets of data in memory

Using MonoDevelop

When we are scripting, we need to use some sort of editor. We could use a standard text editor and achieve great results. But instead of using a text editor, programmers typically use a scripting editor. Scripting editors use color-coding that make the code more readable. They also provide spacing that makes looking at code blocks easier.

The good news is that Unity comes with MonoDevelop. It can handle all of Unity's supported languages (C#, JavaScript, and Boo). MonoDevelop has code completion support and other tools that make scripting more efficient.

You'll gain experience with MonoDevelop in the next section.

Scripting with C# in Unity

Let's get our feet wet by jumping right in and start scripting. The following are the steps to create a new script in Unity using C#:

1. Launch Unity.

2. Open the game project.

3. From the top menu, navigate and select **Assets** | **Create** | **C# Script**.

4. You'll see the script in the **Project** view and you'll be in script name edit mode. Name the script testScript. We'll delete this script when we are finished:

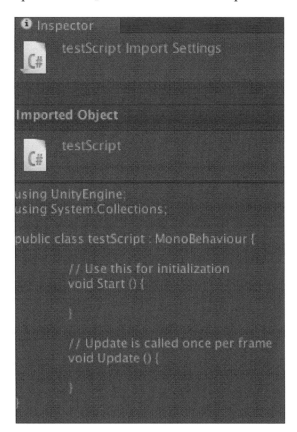

The script is now visible in the **Inspector** view.

5. In the **Project** view, under **Assets**, double-click on the script. This will launch MonoDevelop and provide you with the ability to edit the script:

```
testScript.cs                    ×
No selection
 1 using UnityEngine;
 2 using System.Collections;
 3
 4 public class testScript : MonoBehaviour {
 5
 6     // Use this for initialization
 7     void Start () {
 8
 9     }
10
11     // Update is called once per frame
12     void Update () {
13
14     }
15 }
```

6. Add the following line of code in MonoDevelop in line 8:

```
print("Hello Little Farmer Colt!");
```

7. Your script should now match the following screenshot:

```
testScript.cs                    ○
No selection
 1 using UnityEngine;
 2 using System.Collections;
 3
 4 public class testScript : MonoBehaviour {
 5
 6     // Use this for initialization
 7     void Start () {
 8         print ("Hello Little Farmer Colt!");
 9     }
10
11     // Update is called once per frame
12     void Update () {
13
14     }
15 }
```

8. In the MonoDevelop top menu, navigate and select **File | Save** or **File | Save All**.

9. Close the MonoDevelop window.

10. Review the script using the **Inspector** view to ensure that your changes were saved, as shown in the following screenshot:

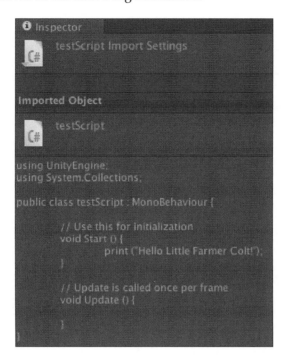

11. Click on the **Main Camera** option in the **Hierarchy** view.

12. In the **Project** view, single-click on the script and drag it to the **Main Camera** option in **Hierarchy** view. This attaches the script to the **Main Camera** option. For scripts to be used in your game, they must be attached to a game object.

13. With the **Main Camera** option selected in **Hierarchy** view, you'll see the script listed as a component in the **Inspector** view:

14. Next, click on the play button. The script was executed and the output message was written to Unity's console pane. You'll find this in the lower-left corner of the Unity interface:

You can also access the output console by navigating and selecting the **Window |
Console** menu option. This will bring up the console in a separate window, as shown
in the following screenshot:

If you followed these steps using the Little Farmer Colt game project, you'll want
to delete the script. The following are the steps to completely delete the test script
we created:

1. In **Hierarchy** view, select the **Main Camera** object.
2. In **Inspector** view, click on the cogwheel to the right of the script object.
3. Select **Remove Component**.
4. In the **Project** view, right-click on the script. Click on **Delete**.
5. Click on the **Delete** button in the pop-up window, as shown in the
   following screenshot:

Start and update functions

You probably noticed that when we first created our C# script, the script shell had two functions:

```
void Start () {     }
void Update () {     }
```

We put our line of code in the Start function so that it would run the first time the object it is attached to is initiated. The **Main Camera** option is initiated when the game starts.

If we print our statement in the Update function, it will be run every frame. Our game is set for several frames per second, so that would be a lot of unnecessary output and processing.

Scripting example

Let's look at a larger script to complete our overview of scripting in Unity. The script you see in the following code is used to get user input via keyboard buttons. It is okay if you do not fully understand this script. It is presented here so that you can gain an appreciation for how scripts look in Unity. This is not something you need to type or add to your game:

```
using UnityEngine;
using System.Collections;

public class ButtonInput : MonoBehaviour
{
    public GUITexture graphic;
    public Texture2D standard;
    public Texture2D downgfx;
    public Texture2D upgfx;
    public Texture2D heldgfx;

    void Start()
    {
        graphic.texture = standard;
    }

    void Update ()
    {
        bool down = Input.GetButtonDown("Jump");
        bool held = Input.GetButton("Jump");
```

```
        bool up = Input.GetButtonUp("Jump");

        if(down)
        {
            graphic.texture = downgfx;
        }
        else if(held)
        {
            graphic.texture = heldgfx;
        }
        else if(up)
        {
            graphic.texture = upgfx;
        }
        else
        {
            graphic.texture = standard;
        }

        guiText.text = " " + down + "\n " + held + "\n " + up;
    }
}
```

This script contains a `ButtonInput` class that has a `Start` and an `Update` method. The `Start` function is executed once the game first starts. The `Update` method is executed in each frame of the game while it is running. This function is how we would detect the button input associated with "Jump."

As you can probably tell, there are four possible states for this button: down, held, up, and nothing. We do not need to look for the button's nothing state as that is the default—that the player is not touching the button. The down, held, and up states are self-explanatory.

The code is offered here so you can get used to looking at it. Once you start learning how to program in C#, this code will be easier to read.

Unity scripting assets

You already have experience with Unity's Asset Store and might already have noticed that scripting is one of the asset categories in the store. There are thousands of scripts for free or paid that are readily available in the Asset Store.

The following screenshot shows a sample free script from Unity Technologies, the folks that created Unity:

The Lens Flares scripting asset includes sixteen lens flares that you can use in your games. Because the asset is free, you merely need to click on the **Open in Unity** button.

You can save a lot of time by using pre-existing scripts.

Now that you have a basic understanding of the C# language and how scripts are used in Unity, it is time to apply this to our game. We'll do that in the next section.

Scripting our game

Before we dive into scripting our game, we need to do a little planning. We will look at what we want to script and what events we want to trigger those scripts. We'll also determine what our data needs are. Since our game is relatively simple, this will not be a difficult set of tasks.

Script planning

Let's review our game's design to determine what needs to be scripted. We know that the primary action a user will take is to navigate the player character in the game environment. As you've already seen, this has been taken care of for us by Unity. This functionality is already in place with no other programming required.

We'll need to plan for events regarding the player gathering corn and water and feeding the animals.

Gathering corn

We've designed our game so that the player character can collect corn and feed it to the farm animals. The way we will accomplish this is to detect when the player character and the corn game objects collide. While that collision is taking place, if the player uses the `take` command, then corn will be gathered. The following flowchart shows this more clearly:

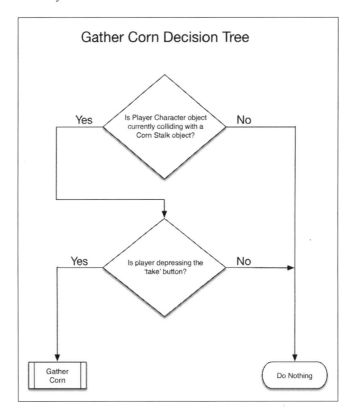

So, we know that we have three scripting tasks to complete:

1. Add a collider so that we know when the player controller and corn stalk objects are colliding.

2. Give the player the ability to evoke the `take` command. We'll program this to the *T* keyboard button. If we were making this a game for mobile devices, we would need a non-keyboard solution.

3. Determine whether the player is using the `take` command while the collision is occurring.

4. Keep track of how much corn the player has.

Gathering water

Gathering water is similar to gathering corn. We'll use a listener to detect the collision and determine whether the player has evoked the `take` command. Then, we'll need to track how much water the player has.

Our scripting tasks for gathering water are:

1. Add a collider for the collision.

2. Determine whether the player is using the `take` command during the collision.

3. Keep track of how much water the player has.

Feeding piglets

The game will start with 10 piglets on Colt's farm. In order for them to grow, they will need water and corn. We will not program any consequences for not feeding the piglets, but will not reward this inaction either. We will set our piglets to grow into adult pigs after they have been given five units of corn and five units of water.

The following diagram shows how the process will work:

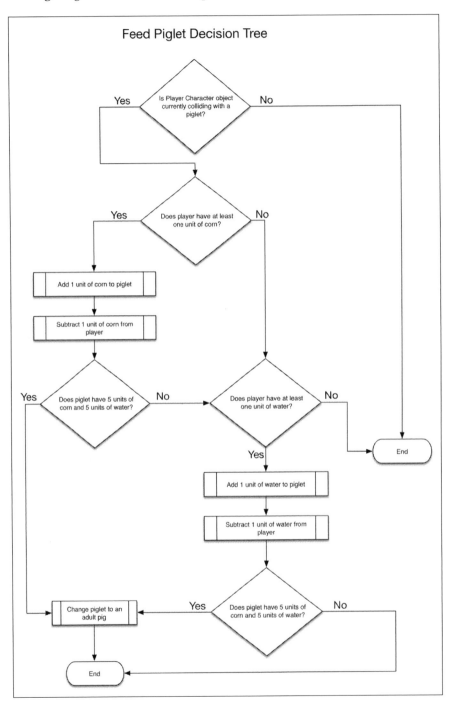

It might look like a complicated process, but feeding the piglets will be an easy scripting task.

Feeding baby chicks

Feeding the baby chicks will work exactly as the process works for the piglets. We'll let the baby chicks grow into adult chickens after they have 5 units of water and 5 units of corn.

For both sets of animals, we will handle the transformation from child to adult in the same manner. When a piglet has been given 5 units of corn and 5 units of water, we will reveal an adult pig at the same X, Y, and Z coordinates of the piglet. Then, we will hide the piglet. This will show a quick change. We'll do the same thing to turn a baby chick into an adult chicken.

Feeding pigs

Once a piglet has been transformed into an adult pig, the pig will start with a count of zero units of corn and zero units of water. The pig will need 10 units of corn and 10 units of water to become a blue ribbon pig. The pigs can consume water and corn beyond 10 units each, so we will not need to limit them.

Achieving blue ribbon status for a specific number of pigs and chickens will be the player's goal.

To script the feeding of the pigs, we'll mimic what we did for the piglets.

Feeding adult chickens

Feeding adult chickens will work in the same manner as for the adult pigs. Chickens will achieve blue ribbon status once they have been fed 10 units each of water and corn. Again, there will be no limit on their consumption.

Data requirements

It is important for us to think about what data requirements our game will require before we start programming. We start by conceptualizing at a high level. For example, we know we need to track information about the piglets, pigs, baby chicks, and adult chickens. Mainly, we need to know how much they consume. We also need to keep track of how much water and corn Colt gathers and has.

We'll take a closer look at our data requirements and decide what to name our variables.

All about the pigs

There will be 10 piglets and 10 adult pigs. For each of those animals, we need to track how many units of corn and water they have been provided. The following table shows the ranges for each data element:

Animal	Visible	Corn	Water
piglet1	Y or N	0, 1, 2, 3 . . .	0, 1, 2, 3 . . .
pig1	Y or N	0, 1, 2, 3 . . .	0, 1, 2, 3 . . .

Based on what you learned earlier in this chapter, you can probably guess what types of data we'll use for each element. The visible element will be Boolean and the corn and water will be integers.

Since this data lends itself well to table, we will use two arrays. One array will be for piglets and the other for pigs. Because arrays use a single type of data, we'll use 0 and 1 to represent non-visible and visible instead of the Boolean data type. The first column will be the sequential number of the animal, so the values will be 0, 1, 2, 3, 4, 5, 6, 7, 8, and 9.

The second column will indicate whether the piglet is visible. A zero (0) will indicate the piglet is not visible and a one (1) will indicate that the piglet is visible. The third and fourth columns will represent the number of units of corn and water respectively.

The following is how we will script the creation of the piglet array:

```csharp
using UnityEngine;
using System.Collections;

public class Arrays : MonoBehaviour {

    int[,] pigletArray = new int[10, 3];

    void Start () {

        for(int i = 0; i < 10; i++)
        {
            pigletArray[i, 0] = 1; // visible: 0=no; 1=yes
            pigletArray[i, 1] = 0; // corn
            pigletArray[i, 2] = 0; // water
        }
    }

    void Update () {

    }
}
```

Line 6 of the **Arrays** script is how we create an array with 10 rows and three columns. Remember, arrays start with zero, so a 10 by 3 array would look as follows:

	0	1	2
0			
1			
2			
3			
4			
5			
6			
7			
8			
9			

In lines 10 through 15, we use a `for` loop to populate the array with initial data. We start by looping through each row of the array starting with zero and ending with nine. Lines 12, 13, and 14 put values into the array. As you can probably see, the first column is set to one to indicate that the piglet is visible. The next two columns indicate that there is zero corn and zero water units.

To see this in action, you can add the following line in between the current lines 14 and 15:

```
Debug.Log ("Piglet " + i + "\t" + pigletArray[i,0] + "\t" +
pigletArray[i, 1] + "\t" + pigletArray[i, 2]);
```

When you save the script, you'll need to drag it to the **Main Camera** option as we did earlier in this chapter. Now, let the game run and watch the output console. You'll notice that there are ten piglets, each with a "1" in the first column, followed by zeros in the remaining two columns:

Now, let's modify the **Array** script to include the adult pigs as well. As you can see with the script in the following screenshot, we essentially replicated what we did for the piglet to take care of the pig-related data needs. We changed `pigletArray` to `pigArray` and set the second column to zero instead of one because the pigs will not initially be visible.

```csharp
using UnityEngine;
using System.Collections;

public class Arrays : MonoBehaviour {

    int[,] pigletArray = new int[10, 3];
    int[,] pigArray = new int[10, 3];

    void Start () {

        for(int i = 0; i < 10; i++)
        {
            // piglet Array initial values
            pigletArray[i, 0] = 1; // visible: 0=no; 1=yes
            pigletArray[i, 1] = 0; // corn
            pigletArray[i, 2] = 0; // water

            // pig Array initial values
            pigArray[i, 0] = 0; // visible: 0=no; 1=yes
            pigArray[i, 1] = 0; // corn
            pigArray[i, 2] = 0; // water
        }
    }

    void Update () {

    }
}
```

Chicks and chickens

Our baby chicks and adult chickens have the same data requirements as their *Suidae* farm companions. We'll replicate the lines of code we wrote for the piglets and pigs to take care of our feathered farm animals:

 Suidae is the scientific name for the pig family.

```
◀ ▶    Arrays.cs                        ✕
 🅒 Arrays  ▶  No selection
 1 using UnityEngine;
 2 using System.Collections;
 3
 4 public class Arrays : MonoBehaviour {
 5
 6     int[,] pigletArray = new int[10, 3];
 7     int[,] pigArray = new int[10, 3];
 8     int[,] chickArray = new int[10, 3];
 9     int[,] chickenArray = new int[10, 3];
10
11     void Start () {
12
13         for(int i = 0; i < 10; i++)
14         {
15             // piglet Array initial values
16             pigletArray[i, 0] = 1; // visible: 0=no; 1=yes
17             pigletArray[i, 1] = 0; // corn
18             pigletArray[i, 2] = 0; // water
19
20             // adult pig Array initial values
21             pigArray[i, 0] = 0; // visible: 0=no; 1=yes
22             pigArray[i, 1] = 0; // corn
23             pigArray[i, 2] = 0; // water
24
25             // baby chick Array initial values
26             chickArray[i, 0] = 1; // visible: 0=no; 1=yes
27             chickArray[i, 1] = 0; // corn
28             chickArray[i, 2] = 0; // water
29
30             // adult chicken Array initial values
31             chickenArray[i, 0] = 0; // visible: 0=no; 1=yes
32             chickenArray[i, 1] = 0; // corn
33             chickenArray[i, 2] = 0; // water
34         }
35     }
36     |
37     void Update () {
38
39     }
40 }
```

We now have four arrays, one for each type of animal.

Corn and water

Our game environment has an unlimited amount of corn and water. When the player gathers corn, no corn is removed from the field. When the player gathers water, no water is actually removed from the river. In a more complex game, we might take a different approach.

So, we merely need to create integers for corn and water. Let's create a new script and name it GameData. You can enter the script based on the next screenshot and then attach it to the **Main Camera** game object:

```
GameData.cs                               ✕

No selection

 1 using UnityEngine;
 2 using System.Collections;
 3
 4 public class GameData : MonoBehaviour {
 5
 6     public int corn = 0;
 7     public int water = 0;
 8
 9     void Start () {
10
11     }
12
13     void Update () {
14
15     }
16 }
```

On lines 6 and 7 of the script, we created public integers of corn and water. We declared the variables and set their initial values with one line of code for each variable. By making these variables public, we can see and change the values in the **Inspector** view:

You can see that the arrays values are not accessible in the **Inspector** view, but the **GameData** values are. This is because we declared the **GameData** variables of corn and water as public. The variables declared in the **Arrays** script are private.

Initializing our data

We have three basic groups of data for our game. The first set is for the piglets and adult pigs. The second set of data is for the baby chicks and adult chickens. Both of these data groups were scripted in the **Arrays** script. Within that script, the data declarations and initial values were in the `Start` function, which means that part of the script will be executed when the object it is attached to is first initialized. Since that script is attached to the game's **Main Camera** option, it will be run when the game first loads.

The corn and water variables, the third group of data, are set in the `Start` function of the **GameData** script, which is also attached to the **Main Camera** option.

> The **Inspector** view shows script names differently than the **Project** view. For example, we created a **GameData** script and it is displayed in the **Project** view correctly. In the **Inspector** view, it shows up with a space in between the two words. All variables displayed in the **Inspector** view will also show up with spaces. Do not be alarmed. Instead, just be aware. It has no impact on the game.

Selective scripts

You can download the full game from the book's web page and review all of the game's scripts. In this section, I'll share several scripts from the game with some explanatory text to help you read the scripts.

Selective script – global variables

The following script is the `GameData` script that we previously created, but with some important changes. You'll remember that we attached this script to the **Main Camera** option in the **Hierarchy** view. Scripts must be attached to game objects or they will not be run.

This script sets up the water and corn variables so that they can be used globally. Each variable is first declared as a `private static int`, with an underscore preceding the variable name. These are our master variables. We can use `GameData.water` and `GameData.corn` to retrieve the current value of the variables.

To make a change to the variables, we can easily increment or decrement them by using a line of code such as `GameData.water = GameData.water +2;` or `GameData. water +=2;`:

```
using UnityEngine;
using System.Collections;

public class GameData : MonoBehaviour {

    private static int _water = 0;
    private static int _corn = 0;

    public static int water
    {
        get { return _water; }
        set { _water = value; }
    }

    public static int corn
    {
        get { return _corn; }
        set { _corn = value; }
    }

}
```

Selective script – evoking the take animation

Our plan was to enable the player to use the *T* (uppercase or lowercase) keyboard key to evoke the `take` animation. The following script does a couple of things to include detecting when the user pressed the *T* keyboard key. That is done by using the conditional `if` attribute and evaluating `(Input.GetKeyDown (KeyCode.T))`.

If the player did press the *T* key, the `take` animation is played. This is accomplished by first declaring the `anim` attribute as a variable type of `Animator`. Next, we create an integer named `takeHash` and set the value to the `take` animation with `= Animator. StringToHash ("Take")`. Now, we can simply reference the animation with `anim. Play (takeHash);`:

```
using UnityEngine;
using System.Collections;

public class Take : MonoBehaviour {

    Animator anim;
    int takeHash = Animator.StringToHash ("Take");

    void Start () {
```

```
            anim = GetComponent<Animator> ();
    }

    void Update () {
        if (Input.GetKeyDown (KeyCode.T)) {
            anim.Play (takeHash);

            GameData.water = GameData.water +1;
            Debug.Log (GameData.water);
        }
    }
}
```

Selective script – feeding the farm animals

Our game will detect when the player-controlled character, Colt, collides with an animal. To do this, we add a sphere collider to each animal. The following are the steps to accomplish that:

1. Select the farm animal in the **Hierarchy** view.

2. From the top menu, navigate and select **Component** | **Physics** | **Sphere Collider**. This will create a sphere around the animal.

3. In the **Inspector** view, adjust the **Radius** of the **Sphere Collider** so that the animal is contained within the sphere, as shown in the following screenshot:

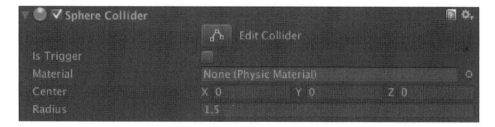

4. Next, in the **Sphere Collider** section of the **Inspector** panel, we need to select the **Is Trigger** checkbox:

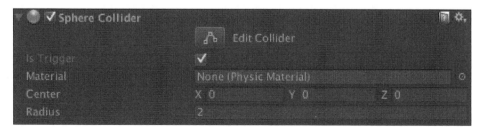

5. Now, we'll script the collider. Create a new script with the **Assets | Create | C# Script** menu selection. Name the script `FeedChicken`, or give it a more appropriate name if you have a different farm animal selected.

6. Edit the script so that it matches the following:

```csharp
using UnityEngine;
using System.Collections;

public class FeedChicken : MonoBehaviour {

    void OnTriggerEnter(Collider other) {
        if (GameData.water > 0) {
            GameData.water = GameData.water - 1;
            // add water to chicken's holdings
        }
        if (GameData.corn > 0) {
            GameData.corn = GameData.corn - 1;
            // add corn to chicken's holdings
        }
    }
}
```

7. Our last step is to assign the script to the game object. With the animal object selected in the **Hierarchy** view, navigate and select the **Component | Scripts | Feed Chicken** menu choice. This will assign the script to the game object. Previously, you did this by dragging the script from the **Project** view onto the game object in the **Hierarchy** view. Both methods work.

 You can program one each of the four farm animals and then duplicate them. This will save you a lot of time.

Organizing scripts

If you are working on large game projects, you might find the number of scripts difficult to manage. There are a couple of tactics you can use to keep your scripts manageable.

The first, and perhaps the easiest, approach is to simply create a scripts folder in **Project** view and keep all of your scripts there. Of course, if you have several dozen or more scripts, you might want to use a folder structure to keep things even more organized.

A second approach is to preface each script file with an identifiable string, such as `script_`. With this schema, our `FeedChicken.cs` script would be named `script_FeedChicken.cs`.

In the **Project** view, there is a list of four **Favorites**, each proceeded with a search icon. Clicking on the **All Scripts** favorites will result in a list of all scripts in the project.

Summary

In this chapter, you learned about scripting with C# in Unity. You gained a cursory understanding of C# fundamentals including syntax and naming conventions. You were guided through the use of MonoDevelop so that you can edit scripts by using the code editor that comes with Unity. The chapter provided insights on how to create scripts and how to attach them to game objects. Using a hands-on approach, you were guided through the creation of your first C# script in our game.

In the next chapter, we'll add a graphic user interface to our game. We'll explore Unity 5's new UI system. We will create and script a full-screen navigational menu, a heads-up display, and a minimap. By the end of the next chapter, you will have created a professional-looking game with a full set of graphic user interface features.

6
Adding a Graphical
User Interface

Our game is nearly complete. One feature that players expect is a **graphical user interface (GUI)**. That is, the set of images, text, and buttons that a player interacts with during the game. We do not want to disappoint or alienate our users, so we'll add some key GUI components to help professionalize our game.

This chapter begins with an overview of Unity 5's **User Interface** (UI) system, followed by a look at game navigation. Also in this chapter, we will create the following GUI components:

- **Heads-up display (HUD)**
- Minimap
- Full-screen navigation navigation

Before we start building our GUI, I'll cover the importance of GUI components and Unity's UI tools.

After reading this chapter, you will:

- Understand the significance of GUIs
- Understand Unity 5's UI system
- Be able to create HUD
- Be able to create minimaps
- Be able to create full-screen navigational menus

An overview of GUI

A GUI is a collection of visual components such as text, buttons, and images that facilitates a user's interaction with software. GUIs are also used to provide feedback to players. In the case of our game, the GUI allows players to interact with our game. Without a GUI, the user would have no visual indication of how to use the game. Imagine software without any on-screen indicators of how to use the software. The following image shows how early user interfaces were anything but intuitive:

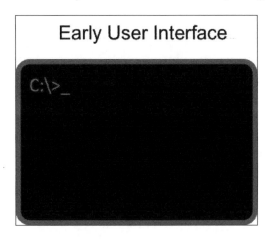

We use GUIs all the time and might not pay too close attention to them, unless they are poorly designed. If you've ever tried to figure out how to use an app on your Smartphone or could not figure out how to perform a specific action with desktop software, you've most likely encountered a poorly designed GUI.

Functions of a GUI

Our goal is to create a GUI for our game that both informs the user and allows interaction between the game and the user. To that end, GUIs have two primary purposes: feedback and control. Feedback is generated by the game to the user and control is given to the user and managed by user input. Let's look at each of these more closely.

Feedback

Feedback can come in many forms. The most common forms of game feedback are visual and audio. Visual feedback can be something as simple as a text on a game screen. An example would be a game player's current score being ever-present on the game screen. Games that include dialog systems where the player interacts with **non-player characters** (**NPC**) usually have text feedback on the screen that informs the user what the NPC's responses are. Visual feedback can also be non-textual, such as smoke, fire, explosions, or other graphic effects.

Audio feedback can be as simple as a click sound when the user clicks or taps on a button or as complex as a radar ping when an enemy submarine is detected on long-distance sonar scans. You can probably think of all the audio feedback your favorite game provides. When you run your cart over a coin, an audio sound effect is played, so there is no question that you earned the coin. If you take a moment to consider all of the audio feedback you are exposed to in games, you'll begin to appreciate the significance of it.

Less typical feedback includes device vibration, which is sometimes used with smartphone applications and console games. Some attractions have taken feedback to another level through seat movement and vibration, dispensing liquid and vapor, and introducing chemicals that provide olfactory input.

We'll include the following feedback GUI elements for our *Little Farmer Colt* game:

- The number of units of corn Colt currently has
- The number of units of corn Colt has gathered in total
- The number of units of water Colt currently has
- The number of units of water Colt has gathered in total
- The number of piglets, pigs, and blue ribbon pigs currently on the farm
- The number of chicks, chickens, and blue ribbon chickens currently on the farm

The following mockup indicates how we will layout the aforementioned GUI elements. You'll note in the mockup that only the top and bottom portions of the screen are represented:

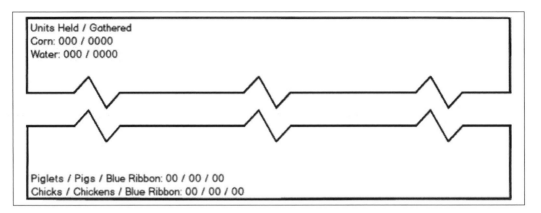

Control

Giving players control of the game is the second function of GUIs. There is a wide gambit of types of control. The most simple is using buttons or menus in a game. A game might have a graphical icon of a backpack that, when clicked on, gives the user access to the inventory management system of a game.

Control seems like an easy concept, and it is. Interestingly, most popular console games lack good GUI interfaces, especially when it comes to control. If you play console games, think about how many times you have to refer to the printed or in-game manual. Do you intuitively know all of the controller key mappings? How do you jump, switch weapons, crotch, throw a grenade, or go into stealth mode? In the defense of the game studios that publish these games, there is a lot of control and it can be difficult to make them intuitive.

By extension, control is often physical, in addition to graphical. Physical components of control include keyboards, mouse, trackballs, console controllers, microphones, and other devices.

We'll include the following control GUI elements for our *Little Farmer Colt* game:

- Keyboard arrow keys control Colt
- Keyboard space bar jumps Colt
- Keyboard *T* evokes the `take` animation and function
- Full-screen game navigation buttons

Feedback and Control

Feedback and control GUI elements are often paired. When you click or tap a button, it usually has both visual and audio effects, as well as executing the user's action. When you click on (control) a treasure chest, it opens (visual feedback) and you hear the creak of the old wooden hinges (audio feedback). This example shows the power of using adding feedback to control actions.

Game Layers

At a primitive level, there are three layers to every game. The core or base level is the Game Layer. This is your game and, in context of this book, the *Little Farmer Colt* game. The top layer is the User Layer; this is the actual person playing your game. So, it is the layer in between — the GUI Layer that serves as an intermediary between a game and its player. The following figure shows the three layers:

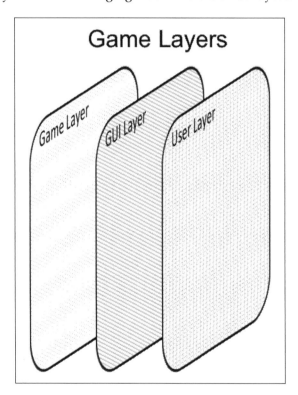

It becomes clear that designing and developing intuitive and well-functioning GUIs is important to a game's functionality, the user's experience, and a game's success.

Unity 5's UI system

Unity's UI system has recently been re-engineered and is now more powerful than ever. Perhaps the most important concept to grasp is the Canvas object. All UI elements are contained in a canvas. Projects and scenes can have more than one canvas. You can think of a canvas as a container for UI elements.

Canvas

To create a canvas, you simply navigate and select **GameObject | UI | Canvas** from the drop-down menu. You can see from the **GameObject | UI** menu pop-up that there are 11 different UI elements, as shown in the following screenshot:

Alternatively, you can create your first UI element, such as a button, and Unity will automatically create a canvas for you and add it to your **Hierarchy** view. When you create subsequent UI elements, simply highlight the canvas in the **Hierarchy** view and then navigate to **GameObject | UI** menu to select a new UI element.

The following table is a brief description of each of the UI elements:

UI element	Description
Panel	A frame object.
Button	A standard button that can be clicked.
Text	Text with standard text formatting.
Image	Images can be simple, sliced, tiled, and filled.
Raw image	Texture file.
Slider	Slider with min and max values.
Scrollbar	Scrollbar with values between 0 and 1.
Toggle	Standard checkbox; can also be grouped.

UI element	Description
Input field	Text input field.
Canvas	The game object container for UI elements.
Event system	Allows us to trigger scripts from UI elements. An event system is automatically created when you create a canvas.

You can have multiple canvases in your game. As you start building larger games, you'll likely find a use for more than one canvas.

Render mode

There are a few settings in the **Inspector** view that you should be aware of regarding your canvas game object. The first setting is the **Render Mode**. There are three settings: **Screen Space – Overlay**, **Screen Space – Camera**, and **World Space**, as shown in the following image:

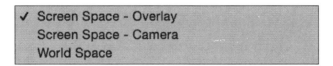

This render mode is the one we'll use in our game. I'll show you how to do that later in the chapter. In this render mode, the canvas is automatically resized when the user changes the size or resolution of the game screen. The second render mode, **Screen Space – Camera**, has a plane distance property that determines how far the canvas is rendered from the camera. The third render mode is **World Space**. This mode gives you the most control and can be manipulated much like any other game object.

I recommend experimenting with different render modes so that you know which one you like best and when to use each one.

Creating a GUI

Creating a GUI in Unity is a relatively easy task. We first create a canvas, or have Unity create it for us, when we create our first UI element. Next, we simply add the desired UI elements to our canvas. Once all the necessary elements are in your canvas, you can arrange and format them.

It is often best to switch to 2D mode in the **Scene** view when placing the UI elements on the canvas. This simply makes the task a bit easier:

 If you have used earlier versions of Unity, you'll notice that several things have changed regarding creating and referencing GUI elements. For example, you'll need to include the using `UnityEngine.UI;` statement before referencing UI components. Also, instead of referencing GUI text as `public GUIText waterHeld;`, you now use `public Text waterHeld;`.

HUD

A game's HUD is graphical and textual information available to the user at all times. No action should be required of the user, other than to look at a specific region of the screen to read the displays. For example, if you are playing a car-racing game, you might have an odometer, speedometer, compass, fuel tank level, air pressure, and other visual indicators always present on the screen.

Our game will have these on-screen elements:

- The number of units of corn Colt currently has
- The number of units of corn Colt has gathered in total
- The number of units of water Colt currently has
- The number of units of water Colt has gathered in total
- The number of piglets, pigs, and blue ribbon pigs currently on the farm
- The number of chicks, chickens, and blue ribbon chickens currently on the farm

Creating an HUD

The following are the steps to create our game's HUD:

1. Open the game project and load the scene.
2. Navigate and select the **GameObject | UI | Text** option from the drop-down menu. This will result in a Canvas game object being added to the **Hierarchy** view, along with a text child item. Rename this item as HUD_Line_1, as shown in the following screenshot:

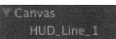

3. Select HUD_Line_1 in the **Hierarchy** view. Then, in the **Inspector** view, change the Text to "Units Held / Gathered".

4. In the **Inspector** view, change the **Font Size** value to 24.

5. Still in the **Inspector** view, change the **Horizontal Overflow** option from **Wrap** to **Overflow**, as shown in the following screenshot:

Horizontal Overflow   Overflow

6. Zoom out in the **Scene** view until you can see the GUI Canvas. Use the transform tools to place the HUD_Line_1 GUI element in the top-left corner of the screen.

 Depending on how you are viewing the scene in the **Scene** view, you might need to use the hand tool to rotate the scene. So, if your GUI text appears backwards, just rotate the scene until it is correct.

7. Navigate and select the **GameObject | UI | Text** option from the drop-down menu. This will add a second text element to the GUI. Rename this item as `HUD_Line_2`.

8. Select `HUD_Line_2` in the **Hierarchy** view. Then, in the **Inspector** view, change the Text to `"Corn: 000 / 0000"`.

9. In the **Inspector** view, change the **Font Size** value to `24`.

10. Still in the **Inspector** view, change the **Horizontal Overflow** option from **Wrap** to **Overflow**.

11. Zoom out in the **Scene** view until you can see the GUI Canvas. Use the transform tools to place the `HUD_Line_2` GUI element just below the `HUD_Line_1` element.

12. Navigate and select the **GameObject | UI | Text** option from the drop-down menu. This will add a second text element to the GUI. Rename this item as `HUD_Line_3`.

13. Select `HUD_Line_3` in the **Hierarchy** view. Then, in the **Inspector** view, change the text to `"Water: 000 / 0000"`.

14. In the **Inspector** view, change the **Font Size** value to `24`.

15. Still in the **Inspector** view, change the **Horizontal Overflow** option from **Wrap** to **Overflow**.

16. Zoom out in the **Scene** view until you can see the GUI Canvas. Use the transform tools to place the `HUD_Line_3` GUI element just below the `HUD_Line_2` element. Your **Canvas** should look similar to the following screenshot (zoomed in top-left corner):

17. Next, we'll create four more GUI elements using the **GameObject | UI | Text** menu selection.

18. Rename the four new text elements as `HUD_Line_4a`, `HUD_Line_4b`, `HUD_Line_5a`, and `HUD_Line_5b`. These elements will be used as indicated in the following illustration:

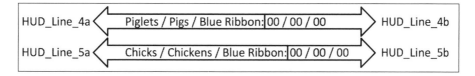

When completed, your **Canvas** object should look like the following in the **Hierarchy** view:

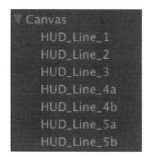

 The previous image shows the **Canvas** child objects. They are also representative of render order, which indicates which order they will be displayed on the canvas. It is possible to have gameobjects overlap or cover another. This should be considered when deciding on placing your UI elements.

19. Make the following changes to each of the four text elements created in the previous step:

    ° Change the **Font Size** value to 24

    ° Change the **Horizontal Overflow** option from **Wrap** to **Overflow**

    ° Move the objects so that they are arranged in accordance with the following **Game** view screenshot:

20. Save your scene and your project.

21. Put the game in play mode and see how the HUD looks. You'll see that the HUD elements remain on the screen at all times.

We now have specific GUI text elements to reference in our scripts, so that we can control what feedback to provide to the user via the HUD.

Mini-maps

Miniature-maps or mini-maps provide game players with a small visual aid that helps them maintain perspective and direction in a game. These mini-maps can be used for many different purposes, depending on the game. Some examples include the ability to view a mini-map that overlooks an enemy encampment, a zoomed out view of the game map with friendly and enemy force indicators, and a mini-map that has the overall tunnel map while the main game screen views the current section of tunnel.

While we do not necessarily need a mini-map for our *Little Farmer Colt* game, we'll create one so that you can replicate the task in your own games.

Creating a mini-map

The following are the steps we'll use to create a mini-map for our game:

1. Navigate and select **GameObject | Camera** from the top menu.

2. In the **Hierarchy** view, change the name from Camera to Mini-Map.

3. With the mini-map camera selected, go to the **Inspector** view and click on the **Layer** button, then **Add Layer** in the pop-up menu.

4. In the next available **User Layer**, add the name Mini-Map:

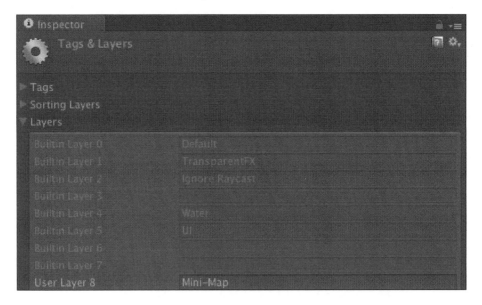

5. Select the **Mini-Map** option in the **Hierarchy** view, and then select **Layer |
   Mini-Map**. Now the new mini-map camera is assigned to the **Mini-Map** layer.

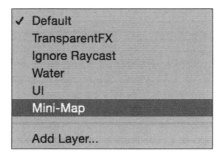

6. Next, we'll ensure the main camera is not rendering the **Mini-Map** camera.
   Select the **Main Camera** option in the **Hierarchy** view.

7. In the **Inspector** view, select **Culling Mask**, and then deselect **Mini-Map**
   from the following pop-up menu:

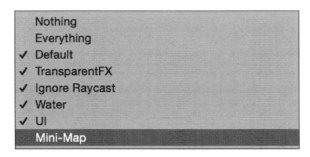

8. Now we are ready to finish the configuration of our mini-map camera. Select
   Mini-Map in the **Hierarchy** view.

9. Using the transform tools in the **Scene** view, adjust the camera object so that
   it is above Colt's farm. Zoom in and out of the **Scene** view as necessary to
   ensure the camera can only see Colt's farm.

10. In **Inspector** view, under **Camera**, make the settings match the following values:

Setting	Value
Clear flags	Depth only
Culling mask	Everything
Projection	Orthographic
Size	25
Clipping planes	Near 0.3; Far 1000

Setting	Value
Viewpoint rect	X 0.75; Y 0.75; W 1; H 1
Depth	1
Rendering path	User player settings
Target texture	None
Occlusion culling	Selected
HDR	Not selected

11. With the **Mini-Map** camera still selected, right-click on each of the **Flare Layer**, **GUI Layer**, and **Audio Listener** components in the **Inspector** view and select **Remove Component**.

12. Save your scene and your project.

13. You are ready to test your mini-map. Put the game in play mode and you'll see that even as Colt travels to Pa Poo's barn, Colt's farm is visible in the mini-map:

Mini-maps can be very powerful game components. There are a couple of things to keep in mind if you are going to use mini-maps in your games:

- Make sure the mini-map size does not obstruct too much of the game environment. There is nothing worse than getting shot by an enemy that you could not see because a mini-map was in the way.

- The mini-map should have a purpose—we do not include them in games because they are cool. They take up screen real estate and should only be used if needed, such as helping the player make informed decisions. In our game, the player is able to keep an eye on Colt's farm animals while he is out gathering water and corn.

- Items should be clearly visible on the mini-map. Many games use red dots for enemies, yellow for neutral forces, and blue for friendlies. This type of color-coding provides users with a lot of information at a very quick glance.

- Ideally, the user should have the flexibility to move the mini-map to a corner of their choosing and toggle it on and off. In our game, we placed the mini-map in the top-right corner of the game screen so that the HUD objects would not be in the way.

Game navigation

Many games start with a full-screen game navigation menu when the game is first launched. Typical elements on these screens are text, images, and buttons. The text will normally display the game's title and the images will be related to the game. One or more buttons are also a normal UI element on main game screens. A very simple game might have a single **Play** button, while more complex games can have several buttons such as play, mode, level, instructions, campaign, and more.

We do not need a fancy game menu screen to allow the user to navigate between scenes or levels. It is important to be able to create these types of screens for more complex games, so we'll dive into this a bit and add a functional button to our existing HUD canvas.

By performing the following steps, we will create a new scene to our game. This will be the main scene that shows a play button. When a user clicks on the play button, the farm scene will be loaded:

1. Save the current scene and the project.
2. Select **File** | **New Scene** to create a new scene.

3. Save the new scene as _MainScene. Let Unity store the scene in the Assets folder, which will be the default location.

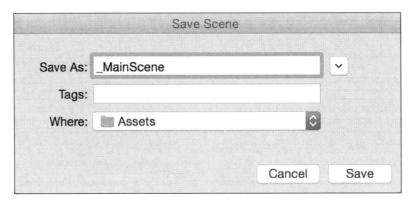

I begin the names of all my scenes with an underscore (_) so that they always show up at the top of the Project view. Alternatively, if you have a lot of scenes, you can create a **Scenes** folder in **Project** view. Keeping your project organized will save you a lot of time and frustration. For larger games, you'll probably want to name your scenes with sequential numbering, such as 01_Main, 02_Jungle, 03_Cave, and so on.

4. You should now be viewing the new _MainScene data with only a main camera and directional light in the **Hierarchy** view. Do not worry, all your _FarmScene data is still intact.

You can easily switch between scenes by double-clicking on the scene name in the **Project** view. If you have any unsaved edits on the current scene, Unity will ask you if you want to save or abandon the edits.

5. Next, select the **File | Build Settings** menu choice to access the build settings dialog.

6. Drag both scenes from the **Project** view to the **Scenes in Build** box of the **Build Settings** dialog.

7. Drag and drop the scenes so that the _MainScene scene is scene 0 and _FarmScene is scene 1.

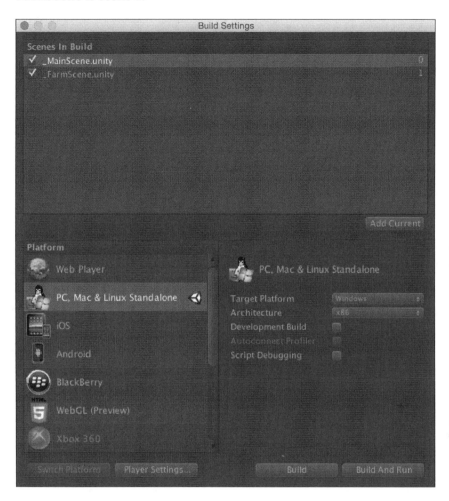

8. Close the **Build Settings** dialog window.

9. Save your project.

   Next, we'll add a button to the new scene that, when clicked, will load _FarmScene.

10. Navigate and select the **GameObject | UI | Button** menu option. This adds a canvas with a child button, as well as an **EventSystem** game object.

11. Expand the button UI element in the **Hierarchy** view to reveal the text component. All buttons have a text component:

12. Rename the button as `Play_Button` in the **Hierarchy** view.

13. Change the text component's text to `Play` in the **Inspector** view. You should now have a **Play** button in the center of the canvas:

14. Navigate and select **Assets | Create | C# Script** to create a new script. This will be our script that is executed when the player clicks on the play button.

15. Rename the new script as `LoadSceneOnClick`.

16. Double-click on the new script to edit it in MonoDevelop.

17. Edit the script so that it matches the following script:

```
using UnityEngine;
using System.Collections;

public class LoadSceneOnClick : MonoBehaviour {

    public void LoadScene(int scene)
    {
        Application.LoadLevel (scene);
    }
}
```

18. Save the script and return to Unity.

19. Drag the new script to the canvas.

20. Select the **Play_Button** in the **Hierarchy** view.

21. In the **Inspector** view, you will see the **On Click()** function at the bottom of the **Button (Script)** component, as shown in the following screenshot:

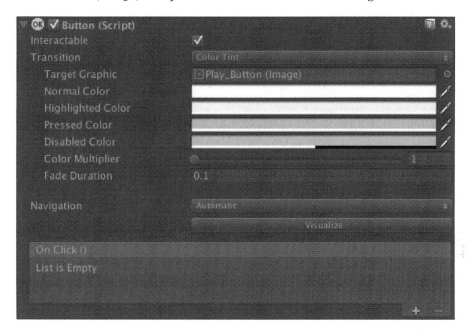

22. Click on the **+** sign at the bottom of the **Button (Script)** section to add a function to the **On Click ()** list.

23. Drag the **Canvas** section from the **Hierarchy** view to the **None (Object)** area of the **Inspector** view, just below the **On Click ()** label.

24. Using the **No Function** pop-up menu in the **On Click ()** area, navigate and select **LoadSceneOnClick | LoadScene (int)**.

25. Our last step is to change the parameter we are passing in to the **LoadScene (int)** function. Change the parameter in the **On Click ()** area from 0 to 1, as shown in the following screenshot:

26. Save the scene and save the project.

Now, when you put the game in play mode, you'll note a couple of changes. First, the new scene we created with only a **Play** button is displayed first. No user actions are possible except to click on the play button. This is our second change. When the user clicks the play button, the farm scene is loaded and the game can be played as usual.

This is arguably a crude implementation of a full-screen game navigation system. Given a little effort, we could add an instructions button that displayed information on how to play the game. We could also add an exit or quit button. If we wanted to spruce things up a bit more, we could add a background image that represents the game. These are just some of the possibilities.

Summary

In this chapter, you learned about the UI system in Unity 5. You gained an appreciation of the importance of GUIs in games we create. As you've learned, there are different types and functions of GUIs. You gained hands-on experience with creating a HUD and a mini-map. You also learned how to create a scene to handle the game's initial load. You walked through the steps of creating a clickable button and scripted the button to load a scene other than the current one. Most importantly, you achieved a level of confidence in creating GUI elements and referencing them in scripts.

In the next chapter, we will look at ways to give our game some final touches. Specifically, we'll add sound effects to breathe life into our game. We'll add shadows to make the game look more realistic. We'll even create some special lighting effects. Our next chapter is about more than just polishing the game; it also contains ways to optimize our game through rendering options and code optimization.

7
Polishing and Optimizing the Game

Okay, all of the heavy lifting is completed. We've completed our game and can play it without running into any errors. You can download the final Unity project from the book's web page. You can extend the game, experiment, and make it your own.

Now it is time to clean things up a bit. Our game needs some final touches to help make it shine. In this chapter, I'll show you how to add audio and visual effects such as sound effects, shadows, and lighting effects. We'll use some of Unity's functionality and explore how we can expand them.

This chapter begins with a brief discussion of the importance of audio and visual effects in games. From that discussion, the chapter shifts focus and shows you how to implement specific effects. We'll start with some key sound effects and then add shadows and lighting effects to our game.

After reading this chapter, you will:

- Be able to add sound effects
- Be able to add shadows to game assets
- Be able to create lighting effects
- Understand how to edit cameras to change rendering options
- Be able to optimize scripts

Sight and sound

Let's try a quick experiment. Sit down at your computer, console, or mobile device and get set to play your favorite game. First, mute the sound. Now, adjust the video settings so the screen is dim and, if possible, black and white. Okay, now play your game. I'll bet the game is not as fun as you remember. Go ahead and reset any settings you changed. Now, play the game again. What a difference!

Even if you did not go along with my experiment, I'll bet you understand the impact those changes would have on your ability to enjoy the gaming experience. This underlines just how important audio and visual effects are for gamers. Imagine an explosion without a sound. You get the point, audio and visual effects are important. So, why talk about them at all? Adding appropriate audio to games is considered a best practice. We'll consider best practices in implementing audio and video in Unity.

Unity's sound capabilities

Unity has great support for playing audio in games. There are a few basics that must be understood before we can start playing audio in our games. First, sounds originate from a source file. Unity supports several audio file formats to include AIFF, MPEG1, MPEG2, MPEG3, OGG, and WAV. One format is not necessarily better than the others. What does matter is if the file is native or compressed.

- Native files are ones that are stored in your game project without compression coding
- Compressed files will take up less disk space but require decompression at runtime, which, depending on the hardware can be enough processing overhead to make your game experience lag

If audio is important to the games you will create in the future, then I recommend exploring Unity's documentation and experimenting with different formats.

Audio listener

Unity creates an **Audio Listener** as a component of a project's main camera. When you select the main camera in the **Hierarchy** view, you can see **Audio Listener** listed in the **Inspector** view.

Audio listeners are simple components without any properties. Ideally, you'll only have one audio listener at a time. For our game, we want the audio listener to be attached to the main camera, which, as you'll remember, we attached to our third person controller game object. This is how the user will be able to hear audio from their audio output device such as computer speakers.

Audio clips

In Unity, we reference an audio source file as an instance of an audio clip. Audio clips are variable types. They are flexible so that we can use essentially any audio type.

The final version of our *Little Farmer Colt* game has a **Pigs Crying** audio asset. The source file is a WAV. When viewed in the **Inspector** view, you can see there are a few settings that we can change:

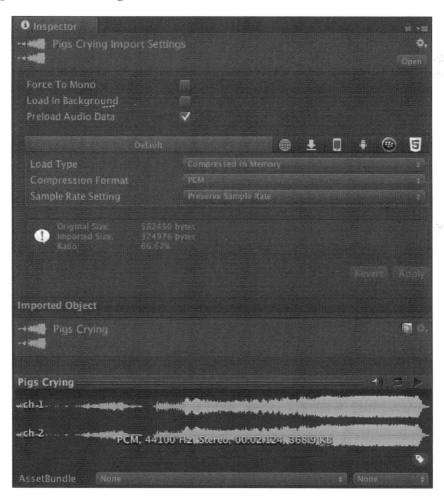

We can, for example, select **Force To Mono**, which will reduce the audio file in the compiled game.

 Unity supports mono and stereo. Mono audio is when a single channel of audio is used, while stereo has two channels. With mono audio, the same sound is sent to both left and right speakers. Stereo audio can be used to send different channels to each speaker simultaneously.

Audio source

One of the things we need to do is to add an audio source to our main camera. We accomplish this with the following steps:

1. Select **Main Camera** in the **Hierarchy** view.

2. In the **Inspector** view, click on the **Add Component** button.

3. Navigate and select **Audio | Audio Source**. This will add an **Audio Source** component to the main camera, as shown in the following screenshot:

4. Next, we'll drag the `Pigs Crying` audio file to the **AudioClip** field of **Audio Source** in the **Inspector** view.

5. Select the **Play on Awake** checkbox. This will start playing the audio clip as soon as the main camera is instantiated.

6. Select the **Loop** checkbox. This will endlessly play the audio clip.

You can play the game now and see that the piglet's sound is constant.

One of the important settings in the **Inspector** view is an audio source's priority. By default, it is set at **128**, which is right in the middle of the high and low ends of the spectrum. When there are multiple sounds for Unity to play, it uses the priority of each to determine which sounds get played. The lower the number is, the higher the priority will be. The following screenshot shows the Audio Source's **Priority** option:

Implementing sound effects

In addition to attaching sounds to an audio source and selecting **Play on Awake** and **Loop**, we can implement sounds via a script. To demonstrate this, deselect the **Play on Awake** and **Loop** checkboxes. Then, perform the following steps:

1. Update the `Take.cs` script to match the following. There are four new lines of code to add, each with a `// new line` comment following the line of code:

```
using UnityEngine;
using System.Collections;

public class Take : MonoBehaviour {

    Animator anim;
    int takeHash = Animator.StringToHash ("Take");

    public AudioClip points;        // new line
    private AudioSource source;     // new line


    void Start () {
        anim = GetComponent<Animator> ();

        source = GetComponent<AudioSource> ();  // new line
    }

    void Update () {
        if (Input.GetKeyDown (KeyCode.T)) {
            anim.Play (takeHash);

            GameData.water = GameData.water +1;

            source.PlayOneShot (points);        // new line
        }
    }
}
```

The new lines of code add a sound effect each time the player presses the *T* key.

2. Next, select **ThirdPersonController** in the **Hierarchy** view.

3. In the **Inspector** view, drag the **Points** audio file from the **Project** view to the **Points** field in the **Take (Script)** area of the **Inspector** view:

4. With **ThirdPersonController** still selected in the **Hierarchy** view, click on the **Add Component** button in the **Inspector** view.

5. Select **Audio | Audio Source**.

6. Uncheck the audio source's **Play on Awake** checkbox. This will stop the clip from automatically playing when the game loads.

Now, every time Colt's `take` animation is played, the "points" audio clip is also played.

Visual effects

There are several ways to bring attention to objects in a game including visual effects. This section will take you through the following examples:

*   Spotlight orb with halo effect
*   Casting shadows
*   Trail rendering

Spotlight orb with halo effect

When you take a closer look at the sign on Colt's barn, you see that it is nondescript:

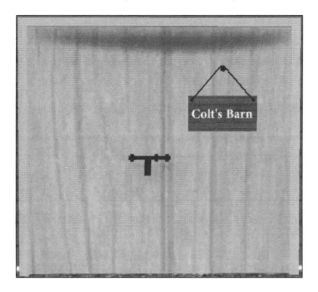

Let's add a spotlight orb and add a halo effect to it:

1. Select **Materials** in the **Project** View.
2. From the top menu, navigate and select **Assets | Create | Material**.
3. Rename the new material `Mat_Yellow`.
4. With the `Mat_Yellow` asset selected in the **Project** view, change the color from the default white to a bright yellow.
5. From the top menu, navigate and select **GameObject | 3D Object | Sphere**.
6. Rename the sphere as `SignLight`.
7. Move the `SignLight` sphere above Colt's barn sign and flush with the door.
8. Resize the sphere so that it looks appropriate on the door.

9. With the `SignLight` sphere selected in the **Hierarchy** view, drag the `Mat_Yellow` asset to the **Mesh Renderer | Materials | Element 0** field in the **Inspector** view.

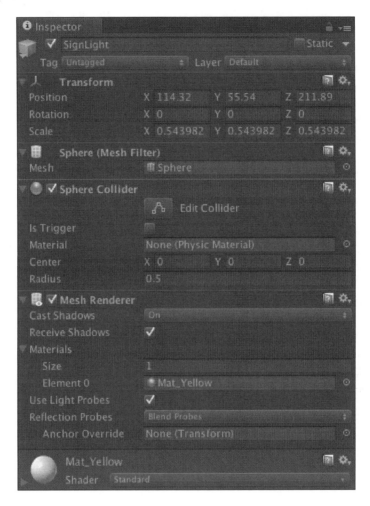

Now that the orb is created, we are ready to create the spotlight.

10. Navigate and select **GameObject | Light | Spotlight** from the top menu.

11. In the **Hierarchy** view, drag the **Spotlight** section to make it a child of the **SignLight** section, as shown in the following screenshot. While this is not necessary, it provides an extra layer of organization to our project:

12. Move the **Spotlight** section in the **Scene** view so that the spotlight appears to be inside the sphere.

13. Rotate the **Spotlight** section so the light shines appropriately on the sign.

14. With the **Spotlight** section selected, change **Range** to 3 in the **Inspector** view.

15. Also in **Inspector** view, change the color to the same bright yellow that you used for the **Mat_Yellow** asset.

16. Select the **Draw Halo** checkbox.

17. Save the scene and the project.

18. Test the new visual effect in play mode.

Casting shadows

You might have noticed that all of our trees cast shadows, but our animals, player, and barns do not. The **Terrain**, by default has the **Cast Shadows** setting enabled. This accounts for the larger mountains that are casting shadows in our scene:

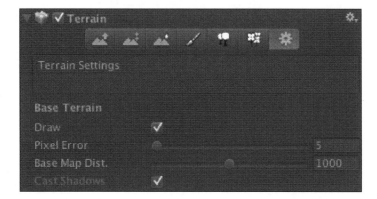

The trees are also casting a shadow. This originates from the directional light we have in the scene. You can simply disable the directional light by deselecting it in the **Inspector** view:

What if we want our two farmers and farm animals to cast shadows? We can add shadows to each game object with two steps:

1. Navigate and select **Farmer | Character1_Reference | Farmer** in the **Hierarchy** view, as shown in the following screenshot:

2. Navigate and select the **Shader | Legacy Shaders | Diffuse** option in the **Farmer-texture** section of the **Inspector** view, as shown in the following screenshot:

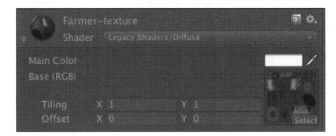

Now, you can see that Pa Poo, our old farmer, casts a shadow. Watch his animations and you'll see that the shadow is dynamic.

Trail rendering

We can create a visual effect in Unity that shows a trail behind an object as it moves. Like a ship leaving a wake, a trail shows where an object has been, in what direction it is heading, and an indication of speed. This is not a feature that we need in our game, but you could easily use this in other games you create. So, we'll demonstrate it with our Colt character. To do so, perform the following steps:

1. Select **ThirdPersonController** in the **Hierarchy** view.
2. In the **Inspector** view, click on the **Add Component** button.

3. Next, navigate and select the **Effects | Trail Renderer** pop-up menu option, as shown in the following screenshot:

4. In the **Inspector** view, set **Cast Shadows** to **on**. This will allow the rendered trail to cast shadows. The actual shadows will depend on the size of the trail, as well as its locational relation to light sources.

5. Ensure the **Receive Shadows** checkbox is checked. With this setting, you can determine whether or not the rendered trail can receive shadows. This can add a level of realism to your game.

6. Drag the Mat_Yellow asset to the **Materials | Element 0** field to apply the bright yellow material to the trail:

7. You can now test the visual effect by putting the game in play mode.

You'll see that Colt is leaving a yellow trail behind him. The arc in the screenshot shows where Colt jumped:

There are a few other **Trail Renderer** settings to consider:

Setting	Description
Time	Here, you set the length of the trail. The value refers to seconds.
Start width	The width size of the trail at the start position. This would be at Colt's feet.
End width	The width size of the trail at the end position. This would be the bitter end of the trail.
Autodestruct	You can set your object to autodestruct after it has been idle for the number of seconds you have in the **Time** setting.

To become completely familiar with this visual effect, I recommend saving your scene, saving your project, and experimenting.

If you employ the **Autodestruct** function of the **Trail Renderer**, your object will be destroyed after the number of seconds you specify in the **Time** setting. If your **Trail Renderer** is attached to Colt, you'll see him autodestruct after he is idle. So, this feature is great for things like sparks and fireballs, but not for our main character.

To disable this effect, simply uncheck the **Trail Renderer** component in the **Inspector** view.

Rendering options

As you know, rendering is the act of creating a 3D image from images, colors, and shading. In other words, creating a visual presentation. Depending on your game, this can be a lot of work for the Unity engine. We can keep our eye on this by selecting **Window | Profiler** from the top menu. This brings up the **Profiler** window.

The Profiler window

The **Profiler** window gives us a view of CPU usage, rendering, memory, audio, physics, and physics (2D). Reviewing these areas can help us determine how our game is performing and where there are potential areas to optimize. We'll focus on the **Rendering** section:

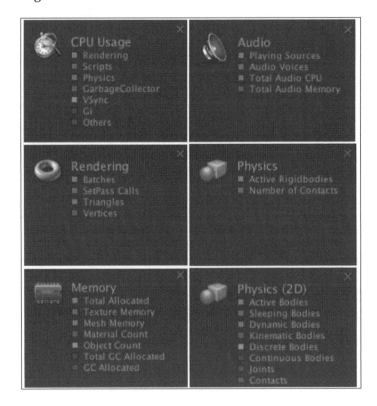

You can switch between any of these Profiler areas. To look at **Rendering**, select that from the left pane of the **Profiler** window. When you put the game in play mode and start navigating the world, the Rendering area of the **Profiler** window will start to populate, as shown in the following screenshot:

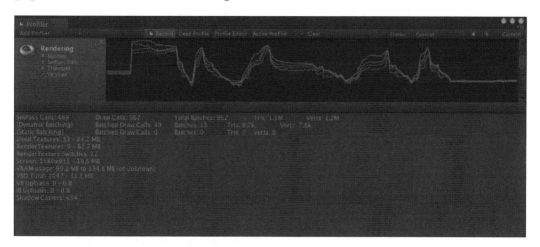

In addition to the color-coded charting that happens on the top portion of the **Profiler** window, very specific rendering information is provided in text format in the bottom section.

Rendering optimization

There are a few things that we can do to decrease the processing overhead related to rendering during game play. Perhaps the most important concept is that realism is costly. We might want to create the most photo-realistic game, and Unity can help us do that. Some of the problems we are likely to run into are game file size, lag, and hardware constraints, for example:

- File size might only be an issue if you are deploying your game digitally or if you are submitting it to a mobile app store that has a file size limit

- The lag issue comes into play when you overstress processing capability or run into bandwidth limitations based on the user's network limitations

- The final issue is of potential hardware constraints. Mobile devices have impressive processing capabilities, but they still underperform when compared to consoles and desktop computers. For example, the issues of alpha transparency and the number of draw calls are important considerations when developing for mobile devices

Imposing limits

The following are a few techniques you can use to help reduce the rendering processing overhead and time:

- Avoid or limit the use of in-game fog
- Limit the use of dense particle effects
- Limit shadows
- Limit reflections
- Use light maps instead of dynamic lighting

Baking images

Another important concept to grasp is the baking of images. We can use baked images to simulate shadows and depth. Using images such as the one for the Colt character in the following screenshot, we can bake special features into the core artwork. This mitigates the need for shadows and lighting effects:

Software such as Photoshop can be used to bake lighting into our 3D models and objects. One technique is to create the lighting effects on a separate layer and then export the final artwork with all layers.

Optimizing scripts

We want our scripts to be optimal in regards to memory usage and processing. A great approach to script optimization is to simply code your game and run it with the **Profiler** window open and select the **CPU Usage** tab from the left pane, as shown in the following screenshot:

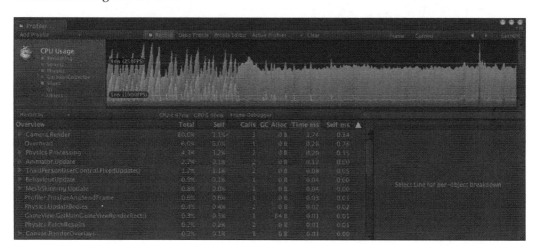

Using this view, you can see what processes are taking the most CPU power. The visual graph makes it easy to spot significant jumps in CPU usage. The **Overview** section, which can be found below the visual graph, provides a very detailed view of how much CPU processing is allocated to each object and process.

Another section of the **Profiler** window is the **Memory** tab. Reviewing that tab's information can tell you how much memory is allocated, how much system memory is used, and counts of **Textures, Meshes, Materials, AnimationClips, AudioClips, Assets**, and **GameObjects**:

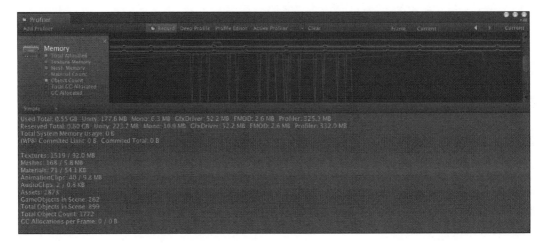

Once we know where our problems or potential issues are, we can do a few things to optimize our scripts:

- We can destroy objects that we no longer need with
  `Destroy(theGameObject)`. Of course, if you intend to reuse the object, think twice about destroying it, as it will take additional processing and can, in some circumstances, result in game lag.

- If we have an object that we need to exist but it does not currently hold a value, we can set the value to null with `theGameObject = null`.

There are other, more advanced techniques to optimize Unity scripts. There is a nice section of the online Unity Manual that references this.

Summary

In this chapter, we have looked at the importance of audio and visual effects as a method of enhancing the gaming experience for our users. We explored Unity's capabilities to help us manage audio with audio listeners, audio clips, and audio sources. We put our new knowledge into practice and add two sound effects to our game: pigs crying and a "points" sound that is played when our game character picks up an item. We looked at visual effects included implementing a spotlight orb with halo, casting shadows, and trail rendering.

We also looked at how to optimize our game with **Rendering** settings. You were introduced to Unity's **Profiler** window and how to read the **Rendering**, CPU usage, and memory data. You learned about rendering optimization and the specific techniques of imposing limits and baking images.

Lastly, we looked at script optimization to ensure our game performs well.

In the next, final chapter, we'll look at what you can do to improve our *Little Farmer Colt* game, the Unity workflow, how to scale projects, physics with collisions, and some cross-platform considerations. We'll also look at a few advanced topics including versioning control and file management.

8
What's Next?

With our *Little Farmer Colt* game fully developed, we can look at ways you can improve the game once you put the book down. You'll gain inspiration to make the game your own with additional content, functionality, and levels.

In the second section of this chapter, we'll look at project-related issues including workflow with Unity projects and how to scale projects. In the third section, we'll look at development issues including cross-platform considerations, plug-ins, and attribution issues.

In the chapter's final section, we'll look at several advanced topics including particle systems, an inventory control system, and a dialog system.

After reading this chapter, you will:

- Understand ways to improve the *Little Farmer Colt* game
- Understand Unity's workflow
- Understand how to scale projects
- Understand cross-platform issues
- Understand the importance of attribution
- Have an appreciation for advanced topics

Improving our game

We can be proud of our game, but there is not much for a game player to get excited about once they've played the game for a while. Here are some suggestions to make our game more robust and more enjoyable for users to play.

Audio

Together, we added sound effects for pigs crying and a "points" sound when Colt takes corn or water. The following are some opportunities for additional audio in the game:

- **Background music**: A subtle background clip played on a loop will go a long way to making the game more immersive. We created something that is appropriate for the game environment. Be sure to review the priorities you set for each audio clip.

- **Animal sound effects**: Ideally, each animal could have three sounds, idle, eating, and drinking. The "pigs crying" sound effect we already added to our game would work for the pig and piglet idle clips. Adding the additional sound effects will help make the game seem more real and add an element of fun.

- **Old farmer**: Currently, the old farmer has several animations. One of these animations is talking. Perhaps an audio clip could be added that sounds muffled. This technique shows that the NPC is talking, but the actual words are indiscernible.

- **Water**: Our game has a large body of water that we've set up as a hazard and a resource. So, Colt can fall into the water and he can retrieve water. This gives us the opportunity to add two water-related sound effects; a water splash when Colt falls in the water and another sound when Colt is taking water.

- **Colt**: Adding a couple of sound effects to the game's main character will help engender players to the character. When Colt jumps, a "woo-hoo" sound could be played or a soft thud could be heard when he lands back on the ground. Maybe after the player has been running for more than x seconds, his breathing could get heavy.

You can use your imagination to help enliven the game by adding audio clips. Not everything needs a sound effect, so you'll want to keep that in mind as you start experimenting.

Visual effects

Adding visual effects to our game will help make it shine. Other than lighting and shadows, our game does not have any visual effects. Here are some ideas you can consider when improving the visual effects for the game:

- **Water**: When Colt falls into the water, it would be great if a splash were seen. Also, when Colt is submerged, air bubbles would be a nice visual addition.

- **Mirror**: We've made the game with a first person perspective. This means that the players never actually see the character they are playing, Colt. We went through a lot of trouble to create the 3D model and animations, so players deserve to see it. Instead of making the game a third-person perspective game, we can add a mirror to the side of one of the barns. You could accomplish this by adding a reflection probe.

The following are the steps to create a mirror in Unity:

1. Create a cube by navigating and selecting the **GameObject | 3D Object | Cube** menu selection.

2. Using the transform tools, reshape the cube so that it is flat and the size of mirror that is sufficient to fit on the side of Colt's barn.

3. Move the cube to the side of Colt's barn.

4. With the cube selected in the **Hierarchy** view, click on the **Add Component** button in the **Inspector** view, then navigate and select the **Rendering | Reflection Probe** option.

5. In the **Inspector** view, select **Type | Realtime** to have the reflection occur during the game dynamically.

6. Still in the **Inspector** view, navigate and select **Type | Refresh Mode | Every frame**. This will ensure your mirror is continually updated during the game.

7. Rename the cube as `MirrorCube`.

8. Drag the **MirrorCube** section from the **Hierarchy** view to the **Project** view to make it a prefab.

9. In the **Inspector** view, make the following changes to the **Mesh Renderer** section:

   ○ Set **Reflection Probes** to **Blend Probes**

   ○ Drag the **MirrorCube** prefab from the **Project** view to the **Anchor Override** input box:

You might need to experiment with the **Mesh Renderer** and **Reflection Probe** settings to get the mirror exactly how you want it.

Functionality

You can add almost any functionality you want to this game. It just takes assets and scripting. The following are some things that would be appropriate for the game based on what we've done so far with it:

- **Body of water**: Currently, not much happens when Colt falls into the water. We've already discussed audio and visual enhancements regarding the water. For functionality, it would be nice if the player could walk on the bottom of the lake and be able to climb back out. Currently, neither of those actions is possible. To make things even more interesting, the player could have a limited amount of oxygen with an on-screen indicator. This would compel the user to work feverishly to get out of the water. If the player does not exit the water fast enough, they (the game character) could die.

- **Corn**: The corn and cornstalks in our game are somewhat arbitrary. You could add a script to the game so that each ear of corn can only be taken once. Each time the player executes the "take" action, the ear of corn the player is colliding with could disappear (destroy game object).

- **Old farmer option one**: The old farmer character is more than just a pretty face. He is capable of so much more than just standing there and being idle. A good option for this character would be to implement a dialog system so the player character can interact with him. To make this viable, the game would need to force the player to interact with the old farmer before going too far in the game. Perhaps, Colt could start the game with no animals. Once he has a conversation with the old farmer, he could receive piglets and baby chicks.

- **Old farmer option two**: If you are feeling extra adventurous, you can edit the game so that a single player controls both the old farmer and Colt. The player would need to have a way to switch between the two characters. Having two sets of farm animals to tend to will make the game more challenging.

- **Old farmer option three**: The next suggestion is not for the faint-hearted, but is worth considering. You can edit the game so two players can play it at the same time via network or web server. One player could control Colt, and other the old farmer. The game could have two modes: cooperative and versus.

Levels

Our game has a single level that never ends. That is okay, but it would be much more interesting if the game had multiple levels. Each level would need a specific goal and set of requirements before the player can move on. What will the additional levels consist of? That is for you to decide. The following are some rough suggestions:

- Each new level could add one additional farm animal such as cows, horses, and goats
- Each new level could add another resource to gather such as grain, milk, oats, and more
- The number of each type of animal could increase for subsequent levels, making it more difficult to manage
- The size of the farmland could increase with each level

You are only limited by your imagination.

Project management

When developing games in Unity, you'll want to ensure you have a project management plan mapped. The adage of *the larger the team, the greater the need*, is certainly appropriate for developing with Unity. As you've seen with our *Little Farmer Colt* game, the number of assets in even a small project can quickly add up. If you are an indie developer, you do not need to be overly concerned about project management, but if you have two more people on your team, I recommend taking a few moments to determine your project's workflow.

Unity workflow

There is no ideal or perfect workflow for working with Unity. Every team does things a bit differently. So, instead of suggesting a specific workflow, I'll mention a few important parts of any workflow and suggest methods of approaching them.

Art and animation

Typically, the team members that work on art and animation are different from those that write the scripts. It stands to reason that the art and animation team (or teams) should be able to progress with their work while developers are scripting. We can, for example, work on scripting a game's inventory control system without actual item graphics. We can easily create cubes and spheres as temporary or placeholder issues while the art team finalizes their models. This permits two processes to occur simultaneously.

With this example, there would need to be a way for the development team to know when the new art/models are ready. Use of a project management tool such as JIRA or BaseCamp can help. Also, if you are using Unity Pro, you'll have access to **Team License**, formerly known as **Asset Server**. This feature is an asset and version control system. To use the system, you'll need to download additional software from the Unity website, install the software on a server or computer with network access, and administer the system. If you are interested in this, you can learn more from the Unity documentation.

Scripts

If you have more than one person working on scripts, you will want to keep your scripts in a central location for easy access. You can use the tools previously mentioned in this chapter or something as simple as an online file storage system that supports versioning.

Other assets

It is important for everyone on the project's team to understand where assets are stored and what their naming conventions are. Implementing a standardized naming convention for assets is a great way to embed organization. Relying on file extensions is often not sufficient. You can poll your team to determine what will work best.

Scaling projects

Unity has a reputation as being a great game engine for indie developers and small game projects. This is somewhat of a bad rap. Unity can be used for large-scale projects. As with using any other game engine, several issues that need to be addressed include:

- File management
- Asset management
- Level control
- Build documentation
- Data backups
- Milestones
- Version control

Development concepts

There are a few things worth talking about as you make your way through the last couple of pages of this book. The concepts of cross-platform considerations, plugins, and attribution are covered in this section.

Cross-platform considerations

You can create multiplayer games and have users on Android and iOS devices playing with or against one another. To accomplish this, you can use something such as Google Play's games services.

Another consideration is the various screen sizes of mobile devices. Apple has a finite number of mobile devices using iOS, but Android runs on a lot more different screen sizes and resolutions. You do not have to create one version for every screen size. Instead, you'll need to consider relative layouts and flexible dimensions.

As always, test your game on as many different devices as you can and be sure to vary operating system versions, screen sizes, and screen resolutions. In absence of actual hardware for testing, use software emulators.

Plugins

We scripted our game by writing our own scripts in Unity using MonoDevelop. We can also leverage code written outside of Unity. If you've developed or have rights to use a plugin, you can simply place it anywhere inside your project. It makes sense to create an **Assets** | **Plugins** folder in your **Project** view.

One thing about many third-party plugins is that they can take more time to integrate into your game than to simply code the functionality yourself. So, it is worth considering both options.

Attribution

One mistake many indie developers make is to use assets they obtain from the Internet. There are several repositories available including the Unity Asset Store. It is important to ensure you have the requisite permission to use downloaded content in your game.

If you are working on a commercial project, you'll want to ensure your asset comes with royalty-free commercial use clause. If you are not certain, you should contact the source where you obtained the asset.

Just because you pay for an asset, it does not mean you have permission to use it for commercial purposes. Always check with the publisher of the asset to be sure you have explicit permission to use the asset for commercial use.

Advanced topics

This entire chapter could have been named advanced topics. And this section could be additional advanced topics. In this section, we'll take a quick look at particle systems, inventory control systems, and dialog systems.

Particle systems

Unity includes an impressive capability to render particles in games. We use particles to represent dynamic visuals such as fog, smoke, fire, sparks, pixie dust, and more. You can think of particles as multiple tiny images in motion. Think of a fireworks display. They consist of hundreds of tiny lights all in motion. Using Unity's particle system, we can replicate this type of imagery.

To implement a particle system in Unity, navigate and select **GameObject |
Particle System** from the top menu. This will result in a **Particle System** object
being placed in your **Hierarchy**. Reviewing the **Particle System** in the **Inspector**
view shows a host of settings that can be used to change how the particle system
functions and is rendered.

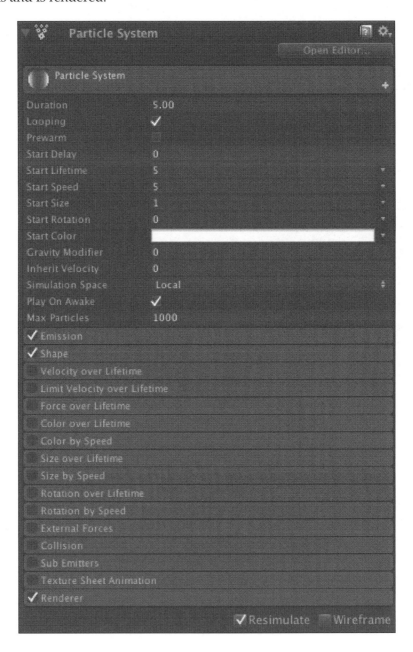

If you plan to implement a particle system in your game, I recommend consulting the Unity documentation for instructional information.

Inventory control systems

Inventory control systems are key parts of a lot of games. Unity does not provide this as a component, so you'll have to either use a third-party plugin or develop one on your own. There are six simple steps to creating an inventory control system:

1. Create a table of all possible inventory items your game will feature. Be sure to record attributes as well.

2. Categorize your inventory items.

3. Mock up the GUI for how your user will interact with the inventory control system.

4. Create the artwork in a standardized way so that all items fit within your GUI.

5. Script the inventory control system.

6. Thoroughly test your system.

Dialog systems

Dialog systems can be fun game components when humanoid NPCs are involved. You do not have to have actual spoken text, but that can be a huge bonus. What is standard is on-screen text with branched answers. It is likely that you've used this feature in many games and are familiar with them. The following are a few tips to keep in mind when developing your own dialog system:

• Map out the entire dialog on paper using flowcharts before scripting. This will help ensure your dialog trees have no dead ends.

• Always give the player an option to end the dialog.

• Ideally, from a user interface perspective, users will not have to scroll to see all the response choices.

Summary

In this chapter, we looked at ways to improve our *Little Farmer Colt* game. Suggested improvements were grouped into audio, visual effects, functionality, and levels. We also looked at workflow project-related issues including workflow with Unity projects, how to scale projects, and how to manage multi-person team projects.

You also learned about development issues, which included cross-platform considerations, plugins, and attribution. We ended the chapter by looking at a few additional advanced topics. Specifically, we looked at particle systems, an inventory control system, and a dialog system.

Enjoy your journey developing games with Unity!

Index

Symbols

3D assets
  creating 46

A

animation clips
  creating 77-81
animations
  about 61, 62
  previewing 75-77
Artificial Intelligence (AI) 22
asset package
  about 46
  creating 47
  importing 48, 49
assets
  about 44
  adding 50
  adding, Unity Asset Store used 50-56
  creating 45
  creating, Blender used 57, 58
  custom asset package, importing 56
  functions 44
  third party assets 44
  Unity assets 44
  user-created assets 44
Asset Server 155
attribution 157
audio
  improving, ways 150

B

Blender
  URL 57
  used, for creating assets 57, 58
bridge
  natural bridge, building 32, 33

C

cameras 17, 18
character controllers
  about 62, 63
  first person controller 63, 64
  third person controller 64-73
C# programming primer
  about 84
  data types 86
  naming conventions 85
  syntax 84
Cross-platform considerations 156
custom asset package
  buildings, importing 57
  game characters, importing 56, 57
  importing 56

D

data requirements, game scripting 97-102
data types, C# programming primer 86
dialog systems 159

E

end states
  defeat 23
  victory 23
environmental features
  about 32
  natural bridge 32, 33
  planting trees 33-36

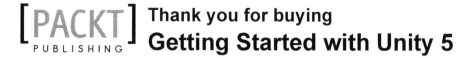

Thank you for buying
Getting Started with Unity 5

About Packt Publishing

Packt, pronounced 'packed', published its first book, *Mastering phpMyAdmin for Effective MySQL Management*, in April 2004, and subsequently continued to specialize in publishing highly focused books on specific technologies and solutions.

Our books and publications share the experiences of your fellow IT professionals in adapting and customizing today's systems, applications, and frameworks. Our solution-based books give you the knowledge and power to customize the software and technologies you're using to get the job done. Packt books are more specific and less general than the IT books you have seen in the past. Our unique business model allows us to bring you more focused information, giving you more of what you need to know, and less of what you don't.

Packt is a modern yet unique publishing company that focuses on producing quality, cutting-edge books for communities of developers, administrators, and newbies alike. For more information, please visit our website at www.packtpub.com.

Writing for Packt

We welcome all inquiries from people who are interested in authoring. Book proposals should be sent to author@packtpub.com. If your book idea is still at an early stage and you would like to discuss it first before writing a formal book proposal, then please contact us; one of our commissioning editors will get in touch with you.

We're not just looking for published authors; if you have strong technical skills but no writing experience, our experienced editors can help you develop a writing career, or simply get some additional reward for your expertise.

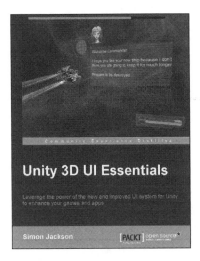

Unity 3D UI Essentials

ISBN: 978-1-78355-361-7   Paperback: 280 pages

Leverage the power of the new and improved UI system for Unity to enhance your games and apps

1. Discover how to build efficient UI layouts coping with multiple resolutions and screen sizes.

2. In-depth overview of all the new UI features that give you creative freedom to drive your game development to new heights.

3. Walk through many different examples of UI layout from simple 2D overlays to in-game 3D implementations.

Learning C# by Developing Games with Unity 3D Beginner's Guide

ISBN: 978-1-84969-658-6   Paperback: 292 pages

Learn the fundamentals of C# to create scripts for your GameObjects

1. You've actually been creating scripts in your mind your whole life, you just didn't realize it. Apply this logical ability to write Unity C# scripts.

2. Learn how to use the two primary building blocks for writing scripts: the variable and the method. They're not mysterious or intimidating, just a simple form of substitution.

3. Learn about GameObjects and Component objects as well as the vital communication between these objects using Dot Syntax. It's easy, just like addressing a postal letter.

Please check **www.PacktPub.com** for information on our titles

Unity 3D Game Development by Example [Video]

ISBN: 978-1-84969-530-5   Duration: 02:30 hours

Learn how Unity 3D "Thinks" by understanding Unity's UI and project structure to start building fun games in Unity 3D right away

1. 2.5 hours of Unity screencast tutorials, broken into bite-sized sections.

2. Create 3D graphics, sound, and challenging gameplay.

3. Build game UI, high score tables, and other extra features.

4. Program powerful game logic with C# scripting.

Getting Started with Unity

ISBN: 978-1-84969-584-8   Paperback: 170 pages

Learn how to use Unity by creating your very own "Outbreak" survival game while developing your essential skills

1. Use basic AI techniques to bring your game to life.

2. Learn how to use Mecanim; create states and manage them through scripting.

3. Use scripting to manage the graphical interface, collisions, animations, persistent data, or transitions between scenes.

Please check **www.PacktPub.com** for information on our titles

Made in the USA
Columbia, SC
24 August 2018